The Elements of Cinema

THE ELEMENTS OF CINEMA

Toward a Theory of Cinesthetic Impact

STEFAN SHARFF

New York **Columbia University Press**

The author wishes to thank the following people
whose drawings have been used as illustrations:

Chris Bryant, John C. Columbus, William H. Hornsby,
Andrea Primdahl, Darcy Ryser and Philip L. Taylor

Photographs for the scene from *The Grand Illusion* used by
courtesy of Janus Films and Compagnie Jean Renoir.

Library of Congress Cataloging in Publication Data

Sharff, Stefan.
The elements of cinema.

Bibliography: p.
Includes index.
1. Moving-picture plays—History and
criticism.   2. Cinematography.   I. Title.
PN1995.S483   791.43'01   82-4268
ISBN 978-0-231-05477-5 (pbk.)

Columbia University Press
New York *and* Chichester, West Sussex

Copyright © 1982 by Columbia University Press
All Rights Reserved
Printed in the United States of America

TO
ALFRED HITCHCOCK

Contents

The Elements of Cinema

Introduction

LEONARDO da Vinci teaches painters how to draw a tree: "if you draw a circle round the crown of a tree, the sections of all the twigs must add up to the thickness of the stem. This lends unity to the tree drawn in full foliage and supplies symmetry to its irregularly shaped branches and twigs." His statement reveals a duality of purpose: it is both a formula and a theory, a method for doing and a way of seeing. It is a craftsman's device and an artist's code.

The present study will look at cinema in a similar way. In demonstrating the existence of uniquely cinematic elements of structure I hope to cast light on cinema's creative processes and on its aesthetic potential. While stressing the primacy of form in cinema as the foremost means for expressing content, I shall endeavor to distinguish between *film* as a medium of mass communication and *cinema* as a potential art form.

In order to understand more precisely what cinema is, one must unravel somewhat the prevailing values and look for principles of visual structure that will define cinema as a craft, with its own laws of aesthetic organization and harmony. To do so requires that a finished film be viewed in a way which penetrates the surface components of plot to delve into the strata of structural elements, the bricks and mortar of cinema.

A large body of writing is devoted to the thematic circumstances of films—its dramatic, sociological, psychological, and political aspects—but there is a persistent lack of clarity about matters strictly cinematic. I shall address myself to the analysis of the "language" of the screen and its internal organization, using as examples a selection of works by the masters of cinema, their followers, and those innovators who successfully helped to formulate this "cinema language."

In the mid twenties, when film matured, a proper cinematic "syntax" began to evolve which employed discernible aesthetic forms: ways of presenting actions through camera placement and cutting which had definable norms. It became apparent that syntax and aesthetics were developing along remarkably parallel lines. This evolution continued, and data justifies the formulation—to borrow from Noam Chomsky—of "rules of competence" and "rules of performance" for cinema.*

Throughout our discussion, I shall often have occasion to mention the audience, and when I speak of cinematic structures, it is essential to bear in mind that they are directed at human viewers endowed with the capacity to understand and be gratified by them. The ability to decipher and follow a cinema syntax resembles the innate faculty for language which is universal in the human species. It is our possession of this faculty which accounts for the ability of film audiences, from the very beginning of movies, to follow a chain of shots and "match" images spread over a considerable span, and thus to draw conclusions from groupings of shots (the filmic "sentences" and "paragraphs"). Cinema thus can claim to be, alongside language, the only other form of communication which exists on a syntactic continuum: a sequence of signs that "make sense" when arranged grammatically and convey meaning on both a literal and an emotional level.

The analogies possible between cinema and language in fact have some depth. Yet as we shall see, they must be constantly reevaluated in light of the unique qualities of cinema, especially its nonmetaphoric vocabulary and its special relationship to reality. Analogies to music are also illuminating, considering the strong modality of cinema, its use of harmonic patterns, repetitions, and symmetries and the importance of rhythmic values. Just as tonal music has discernible principles of modality, key, measure, and harmony, so cinema has its own principles of organization: a succession of images within specific elements of structure. I shall show the existence of recurrent structural patterns and harmonic designs and then define the laws, limitations, and specificity of cinema as a form of expression.

*Chomsky has distinguished between rules of competence (they are the rules which will generate grammatical sentences) and rules of performance (stylistic rules). See Noam Chomsky, *Aspects of the Theory of Syntax* (Cambridge: MIT Press, 1965), pp. 8–15 and *passim*.

As we consider the grammatical phenomena inherent in a proper succession of images on a screen, bear in mind that this visual grammar is still tentative and has not been codified; in fact, its occurrence in films is often unconscious. We must therefore address ourselves to a more or less ideal cinema, a cinema which is nevertheless practiced, at least in part, by a large number of filmmakers—especially the masters.

A few of the elements of this grammar have evolved quite naturally through filmmaking processes Into rules of thumb that can be found in many technical books. I, too, include some of these basic rules, but unlike the "how to" textbooks, I have here set them in the context of a theory of cinesthetic forms. At the same time, this is not a work of polemical scholarship, but is intended to be a theory of cinema from the "artist's studio" perspective. I have accordingly refrained from discussing other film theories, past or present, including the more recent semiotic approach. More importantly, however, while considering the arguments presented here, the reader may have to shift from one style of thinking, which views film editing as the only method for arriving at cinematic solutions (by trial and error), to another, which views language-like constructs as a basis for composing a work of cinema.

I have tried to keep terminology as simple as possible. Most terms are in general use, and those which I have used to identify the elements of structure (separation, slow disclosure, familiar image, and the like) are in the vernacular. They are already familiar to generations of my students at Columbia University film school, and by sheer force of habit I have continued to use them in this book. References to "film grammar" concern the relationships among shots in a sequence, while "syntax" applies to the system by which larger units are organized into structural elements. "Matching" shots, an expression borrowed from linguistics, refers to the viewer's ability to pick up and combine visual signals into units of meaning.

The film sequences I have chosen to analyze represent successful uses of elements of structure, and their analysis here does not necessarily connote a critical judgment of the film as a whole. The drawings used were executed by a few graduate students as part of their course work in my classes and were chosen to show several different approaches to the problem. Photographs are used in one instance, but in my opinion drawings better delineate the essential graphic features of a "frame" without the clutter of unimportant details.

My methodology evolved during more than 20 years of teaching "Analysis of Film Language" at Columbia University, as well as during the more than a quarter of a century of practical filmmaking. Eventually I narrowed down the research to a group of about 300 "basic" films, mostly feature length, for the sake of determining the inner relationship of the arts, to disentangle the essential from the accidental, and to illustrate recurrent patterns. Though I intend to clarify and make vivid my ideas on the subject, I am nevertheless aware that there is nothing quite so tedious as reading a verbal description of what is *ipso facto* a visual experience.

The principles outlined in this book are directed specifically at cinema, yet they apply equally to any succession of images on a screen, including television. It is my hope that they are stated convincingly enough to justify their consideration as "the rules of the game." Although Godard and other recent filmmakers, and a legion of theorists in Paris and elsewhere, have raised new and difficult questions about so-called classical film style, it is my opinion that cinema is still a developing art, which has not yet gone through an anticlassical crisis in either a stylistic or a philosophical sense. It is reasonable to assume that a classical period in cinema will eventually materialize, to be followed by the kind of mutations in form and content which have characterized the evolution and growth of the other arts. While filmmakers of the future may indeed achieve new forms of the kinds dreamed of by novelists and poets, it seems essential first to understand the nature of the cinema as we know it now: what is *its* language and syntax? This study addresses itself to that question. I trust that the reader will be tolerant of my obvious biases, bearing in mind that I am a working filmmaker, teacher, and still-ardent student of cinema.

I would like to thank Ms. Rachel Cox for her many suggestions on points of literary congruity, and I must acknowledge my gratitude to the scriptwriter Samson Raphaelson for his careful reading of this manuscript.

1

On Cinematic Structures

MOST critical thinking about the traditional arts is a matter of post facto analysis of existing works. Cinema distinguishes itself by offering the analyst a look at a contemporary art observable in all its stages of development. This development spans the relatively recent invention of cinematography, its use as a medium of mass entertainment, and the appearance of aesthetic forms of cinema. A study of these forms affords the rare opportunity to chart, from its birth, the evolution of an art.

Of course, there was—and still is—cross-pollination between cinema and the older arts, particularly the novel, the theater, and the plastic arts. Nevertheless, cinema is not a composite of those arts and has its own unique methods of providing aesthetic gratification, which I shall call its cinesthetic elements. It is these elements which the filmmaker organizes into cinematic sentences. (I am implying no precise linguistic analogy, however: shots are not words, and film has nothing like noun-verb structures.)

The unique quality of the cinesthetic elements is that they are repeatable configurations with stylistic and narrative functions which every moviegoer learns how to "read." Each element consists of a grouping of shots formed into a unit with autonomous characteristics. The cognizances of these cinesthetic elements of structure is essential to the recognition of cinema as an art form. Such cognizance will lead to an understanding of "cinema syntax" and the way it operates.

To begin, then, I would like to dissolve the boundary between cinematic content and form by analyzing the artistic methods used in structuring the identified cinesthetic elements. René Wellek's definition of structure in art points the way:

> Structure is a concept including both content and form so far as they are organized for aesthetic purposes. The work of art is then considered as a whole *system* of signs or structures of signs, serving a specific aesthetic purpose.*

In cinema, this system is derived from the artist's choice of the kinds of "elements" of construction to employ and their order and timing, and from his awareness of a total structural design for his film. This process generally involves presenting chiefly linear information (the story) through a battery of shots. Using various cinematic configurations, the artist creates expectations in his audience, which thus elaborates on the given information. The audience is drawn into a decoding cycle controlled by this system. A relationship is set up between screen content and the subliminal interactions of reality and illusion. The result is the mystique of cinema art—cinesthetic impact. By examining the specific elements and their various arrangements, we begin to understand the nature of this impact.

Using the method of shot-by-shot analysis in over 300 selected films, I have isolated eight basic models of structure:

(1) *Separation:* fragmentation of a scene into single images in alternation—A, B, A, B, A, B, etc.
(2) *Parallel Action:* two or more narrative lines running simultaneously and presented by alternation between scenes.
(3) *Slow Disclosure:* the gradual introduction of pictorial information within a single shot, or several.
(4) *Familiar Image:* a stabilizing anchor image periodically reintroduced without variations.
(5) *Moving Camera:* used in scenes without cuts.
(6) *Multi-angularity:* a series of shots of contrasting angles and compositions (including reverse and mirror images).
(7) *Master Shot Discipline:* a more traditional, Hollywood film structure.
(8) *Orchestration:* the arrangement of the various other elements of structure throughout the film.

---

* Rene Wellek and Austin Warren, *Theory of Literature.* rev. ed. (New York: Harcourt, 1970), p. 141.

To some, this numerical classification may seem arbitrary, and there are indeed many possible subdivisions and variations for these models. It is nonetheless helpful to begin by using these designations as if they were a basic eight-tone scale for cinema which allows for many combinations. Although often overlapping and combining with each other, the specific elements retain their strength within their speciality.

Take as a first example the element of separation, an arrangement of shots showing subjects one at a time on the screen, as in a scene of two conversing people shown in alternation.

Separation can accommodate any given thematic situation, but cinematically its specialty lies in the ability to create intimate relationships between *parts* seen *separately* on the screen. This ability makes the element of separation specific in its techno-cinematic laws of structure. Those laws interlock with factors of screen reality. A more realistic alternative to two people talking in separation would be to show them both in one frame. Yet it is the strength of the element of separation that, *seen one at a time*, those people seem in a more intimate "dramatic" contact. Successfully executed, separation can be one of cinema's most effective devices. The audience is drawn to participate in a controlled fashion in unifying the separate parts.

The element of separation, as well as the other cinesthetic elements of structure, operates on both narrative and extra-narrative levels (i.e., levels more elaborate than descriptive), allowing wide latitude for subtle decorative constructions. The most significant of these are film sequence *symmetries* and image *repetitions*.

All cinesthetic elements function in trigger-release fashion, by an alternation between intensity and rest to which *exact graphic forms are essential*. This brings to mind Clive Bell's cryptic phrase: "significant form is the essence of every art." Significant form is especially relevant to cinema, for it is the very source of the cinesthetic element. Significant form is the opposite of pedestrian rendition; it is like seeing something familiar in a new and freshly important light. Because it has great density and energy, significant form conveys narrative information with weight. At the juncture of well-chosen shots with such forms, something mysterious happens which resembles a chemical reaction. Images fit together so magnificently that they ascend to a higher level of visual meaning.

Of course, one cannot speculate on the nature of any cinematic element without considering what comes before and after it. The proposition that any single shot has cinematic value outside the chain of construction is inadmissible, for the most characteristic trait of the film medium is continuity of motion—the uninterrupted run of the film. It is not the moving image, the traveling camera, or the world in motion that is the essence of the motion picture, but rather the flow of a succession of images on a screen—the continuous chain of shots.

Although the syntactic rules for each element of construction are constant, there are many combinations which reflect varying approaches to the problem of cinematic style. On the premise that there are proper methods of construction, the use of these elements must be tested in the context of cinematic reality. There exists on the screen a reality which, regardless of its stylizations, codes, distortions, and arrangements, is ultimately decipherable on the basis of everyday human experience. Often in cinema a balance is struck between that reality and the illusion of reality presented on the screen. The analysis of the elements and the subsequent formulation of laws governing their construction will prove that the creation of cinematic reality involves unique codes. Without proper construction of these elements in a chain, the illusion of the reality—or the reality of the illusion—will collapse (see chapter 2).

Further study of such laws of structure should reveal that narrative continuity in cinema does not depend only on linear development. In a majority of cases, cinematic continuity is nonlinear. Thus one arrives at a total cinesthetic impact not through linearity, but through orchestration of the elements of structure with an imprint of stylistic direction.

Cinema is a storytelling medium, and in building a film directorial decisions aim toward a "drama of the cinema." This is partially true even for nonfictional films. Characteristically, any succession of images on a screen will provoke some notion of a story. Much conventional film criticism evaluates only the quality of the narrative. But cinema has developed far beyond that. It has evolved from photographic storytelling to sophisticated forms of expression. Hence, a distinction can be made between the "easy" *film* and the "complex" *cinema* of stylistic organization. Difficulty in making such a distinction may be partially accounted for by the critic's inability to "read the cinematic text" that lies below the hypnotic effect of the narrative. The masters of cinema—the inventors of cinesthetic elements—proved that *harmonic structures not only improve storytelling technique but also lift it to the level of artistry.*

Perhaps habits in reading film content are still tied to the literary tradition, and its particular systems of structure; cinema cannot and should not compete with the written word. Visual thinking and cinema "language" together must be understood as a different kind of intellectual activity. Cinema is a chain of visual impressions running and interlocking in an uninterruptible succession of graphic bombardments. The laws of expression for conveying an idea in visual terms—its syntax—are unlike the ones we use to organize ideas in the verbal mode; the whole matrix differs. The clarity and force of a visual statement depend on the filmmaker's understanding of how to organize *significant form* into cinesthetic elements so that the result is a dynamic flow of screen information.

In creative cinema, the simplest scene involves a series of directorial decisions that go far beyond the need to communicate the total amount of information of a realistic situation. A detailed analysis of such a scene shows the presence and complexity of cinema structure. A minor scene from Hitchcock's *The Birds* will serve to demonstrate. The scene occurs about one-third of the way through the film, after the bird attacks have begun. Lydia (Jessica Tandy), the protagonist's mother, is on a routine visit to her neighbor Dan. She drives a pickup truck. Upon arrival, she asks a farmhand where Dan is. She is directed to the house. She enters a long corridor and notices broken cups hanging on shelves, a sign of the birds' destructiveness. Entering Dan's bedroom, she is startled at first by a broken window with a dead bird stuck in the glass. Then she sees Dan's bloody legs and eventually the rest of his body. Horrified, she quickly withdraws, running out of the house through the same corridor, jumping into her pickup and rushing toward home.

The scene has 21 shots and is 2½ minutes long (see Figure 1.2). It starts with an extra long shot of Lydia's pickup truck going to the right toward the farm (12 seconds); it ends with a similar shot of Lydia's pickup truck returning to the left (15 seconds). The group of the first and last three shots is approximately of the same length (10–15 seconds). Shots 5 and 6 are the longest (approximately 20 seconds apiece), constituting a pause before the "slow disclosure" of Dan's body. From shots 7 to 17 there is a strong rhythm of short cuts—from 4 to ¾ seconds long—the climax of the scene. Throughout, Hitchcock uses opposite juxtapositions: left-right, high-low, horizontal-vertical (see Figure 1.1). The stroke of genius comes in the center of the climactic shots (14, 15, 16), disclosing the mutilated body of Dan in a three-shot salvo, from medium close-up to extreme close-up and from 1½ to less than ¾ seconds long, a staccato on one axis of view. Without exploring the goriness, this structure leaves an electrifying impression (see analysis, pp. 10–17).

THE BIRDS

Shot 1. 12 seconds. Long shot. Lydia's pickup truck riding to the farm (screen left to right). Real time. First symmetry: with shot 21 (end of scene). A mild beginning that pays off at the end in a similar shot of greater intensity (shot 21).

Shot 2. 11½ seconds. Medium shot of Lydia's pickup truck coming from back of camera to long shot as she parks. Condensation of real time. Second symmetry: with shot 20. Winding up of tension through the sudden intrusion of the truck from the screen foreground. Hitchcock is starting a series of symmetries which reach out to the opposite end of the scene.

Shot 3. 9 seconds. Medium long shot. Lydia walks over to farmhand and asks for Dan. Real time. Third symmetry: with shot 19.

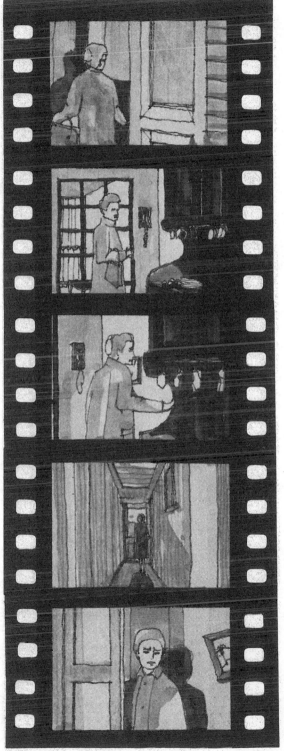

Shot 4. 10 seconds. Medium shot. Lydia approaches door of the house and enters. Condensation of real time. Opposite movement (from L–R to R–L).

Shot 5. 21 seconds. Medium, low level. Inside Dan's house. She looks at the broken cups. The camera tracks into her face and then the cups. Elongation of real time. The camera's tracking in underlines the beginning of suspense. Slow disclosure starts (shots 5–16).

Shot 6. 18 seconds. Medium, low level. She comes out and walks down to the end of the corridor. Fourth symmetry: with shot 18. Opposite movement. The long, narrow perspective walk away from the camera adds tension.

Shot 7. 3 seconds. Medium close-up, low level. Her face distorts at what she sees. Fifth symmetry: with shot 17. Opposite movement.

Shot 8. 4 seconds. Medium, eye level. A dead seagull in the window. The plant is turned over. Narrative resolution starts.

Shot 9. 4 seconds. Medium close-up, eye level. She looks around the room. Separation starts: Shots 9–17. Familiar image in separation: Repeated in shots 11, 13.

Shot 10. 2 seconds. Medium, eye level. The crowded room. No movement. A dead crow on the bed. Tempo increases.

Shot 11. 3 seconds. Medium close-up, low level shot. Lydia's face looking down. Condensation of real time. Familiar image in separation, shot 2.

Shot 12. 2 seconds. Close-up, high shot. The bloody legs. Climax starts. The fragmentation in closeup adds to the suspense.

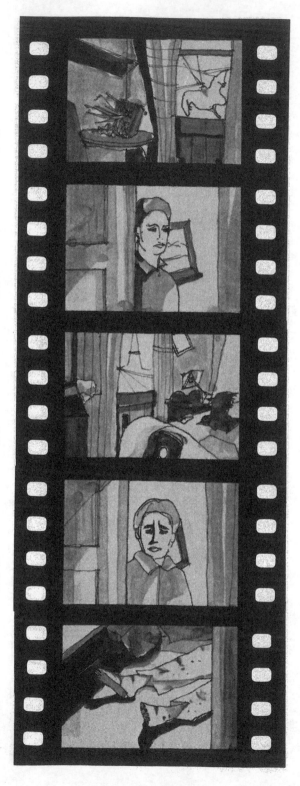

Shot 13. 3 seconds. Medium close-up, low level. Lydia's face is still looking down. Condensation of real time. Familiar image in separation, shot 3.

Shot 14. 1½ seconds. Medium, high. Dan's bloody face. "Drumbeat salvo" of 3 shots (14, 15, 16). They defy the so-called point-of-view tradition. Tempo faster.

Shot 15. 1 second. Medium close-up, less high. This staccato of close, closer, closest is purely cinematic, and not the way a person sees.

Shot 16. 1 second. Close-up—eye level. Dead Dan's face. Peak of climax. Last shot of the "salvo." Slow disclosure (shots 5–16) ends.

Shot 17. 1 second. Medium close-up, low level. Lydia leaving the room. Separation (shots 9–17) ends. Reverse symmetry with shot 7.

Shot 18. 5 seconds. Medium, low level. She is running down the corridor. Condensation of real time. Reverse symmetry with shot 6.

Shot 19. 11 seconds. Medium to close-up, low. She is running away from the house. The camera is tracking to a close-up, of her and the farmhands' faces. Reverse symmetry with shot 3.

Shot 20. 6 seconds. Medium, eye level. Her head comes out the left side of the frame beyond the truck. She turns around and gets into the truck. Reverse symmetry with shot 2. Unwinding of tension.

Shot 21. 14 seconds. Extra long shot, eye level. The truck is moving rapidly back across the dusty road. Real time. Reverse symmetry with shot 1. Opposite movement. Familiar image.

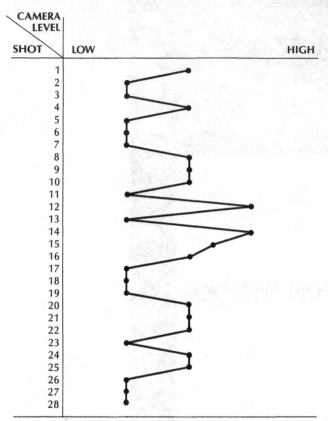

Figure 1.1. Level of shot.

In this brief analysis we have observed the following structural elements:

A. Familiar Image (in repetition).
   2 long shots of the truck arriving and departing (1, 21).
   2 medium shots of the corridor—Lydia coming and going (6, 8).
   2 close-ups of Lydia's face entering from the door frame and window (7, 17).
   2 close-ups of Lydia's face looking (11, 13).
B. Slow Disclosure. From (4) to the climax (12).
C. Multi-angularity. Most of the shots, especially the three-shot climax—which is specifically reserved for the central position in the scene and different in its iconography from the rest (14, 15, 16). Opposite camera movements and opposite graphic arrangement.
D. Separation. Between Lydia and what she sees (absence of "over the shoulder," shots) (9–17).
E. Orchestration. The rhythmical curve of a definite pattern from longer to shorter shots. Symmetries.

To summarize, Hitchcock's scene contains overall symmetry in timing (from longer to very short shots and back to longer), three sets of internal symmetries, slow disclosure, and opposite movements. In the center of the scene the burst of brief shots is the climax of both content and pictorial originality (Dan's bloody body)—an emphatic abstraction from stark reality. The condensation of real time leaves the impression of a longer scene. In the context of the rest of the film this scene is part of an accelerated and well-distributed series of trigger and release sequences. The scene's impact is a result of total orchestration.

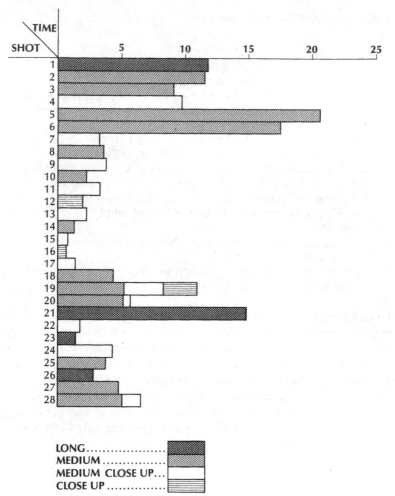

Figure 1.2. Length of shot.

This sample shows how the skillful filmmaker uses a system of structural elements integrated into a pyramidal pattern. The shots are designed to ascend to a dramatic peak and then descend symmetrically, on the other side. The cinema artist is not concerned here with presenting a slice of life; his aim is a cinesthetic *composite* statement (stripped of visual rhetoric) which fulfills both narrative and aesthetic needs. The result is a scene that embodies the economy, strength, and artistry of expression which only a structured cinema can generate.

2
On Cinematic "Syntax"

IN dictionaries, syntax is defined as: (a) A connected system or order, and (b) The due arrangement of word forms to show their mutual relations in the sequence.

Syntax treats word relations according to *established usage,* and adherence to such usage is obligatory. A nonsyntactical sentence has the wrong ring to it and will be rejected intuitively by the native speaker.

Because film images so closely resemble reality, simple communication in film can be achieved without any established "grammatical" order, as when real events are captured in real time by the camera or staged uninterruptedly in front of it. So long as the images are in general conformity with the viewer's experience, they will be understood; and if they do not tamper excessively with such reality, they will be believed.

Quite early in the history of film, however, it was discovered that such "proscenium" photographing of reality inhibited sustained communication. The flatness of the screen and its other limitations led to the conclusion that this new branch of the dramatic arts needed a more active and vibrant form of presentation.

In the search for such a form, filmmakers began to fragment the photographed "proscenium" reality into *shots and sequences of shots.* This circumstance was of paramount importance. From the moment *shots* were introduced, "a due arrangement . . . to show their mutual relationship" *had* to be worked out. Shots were fragments of reality, and the audience—much as was the case with language—had to "match" them in order to decipher the meaning of the sequence. This led to the beginning of a film grammar.

In brief, the earliest stage in this grammatical development amounted to a breaking up of the "wide-angle" view of the world into narrow segments which, when arranged into a sequence, would merge again into an *illusion of the wide-angle reality*. A sequence so arranged had to have the "right ring to it"; otherwise it would not merge properly and would be rejected by the "native speaker"—in this analogy, the average movie audience. Through trial and error, filmmakers unconsciously developed a simple grammar, at the same time starting to condition their audience to accept the usage of new visual configurations.

The initial steps in this process characterize its continued evolution as well. At first, filmmakers were afraid to use close-ups for fear that the audience would not properly connect the giant face on the screen with the same person in the full shot. The first attempts at closer shots were therefore executed in a manner which today would seem comical. In a robbery scene, for example, a long shot of an intruder opening a door would be followed by a closer shot of the same intruder opening the same door all over again (as if to make certain that it is the same door and the same intruder seen previously in the long shot). After observing that audiences understood such switches to closer shots, the filmmakers became more bold in using them. They intuited the innate ability of their audience to be comfortable within a structural organization. First steps toward "grammar" can be seen, e.g., in the films of Lumière and George Méliès (France), and in Ferdinand Zecca's *The Red Spectre* (France, 1903), Edwin S. Porter's *Life of an American Fireman* (USA, 1903) and *The Great Train Robbery* (USA 1903), and Vippo Larsen's *For a Woman's Sake* (Denmark, 1907).

Due credit should also be given to D. W. Griffith for perfecting the initial "film phrases" as the evolution of such forms got under way. It can easily be said that Griffith opened the magic box of cinema's possibilities. His personal contribution was the methodical, consistent improvement of filmic expression—temporal and spatial elements, continuity, the chase, etc. To quote his own advertisement in *The New York Dramatic Mirror* in 1913, his "large or close-up figures, distant views, the switch-back, sustained suspense, the fade out and restraint in expression . . . raised . . . motion picture acting to a higher plane [and] . . . won for it recognition as a genuine 'art.' " By the end of his Biograph period of one-reelers (1909–1912), Griffith's simple grammar had already become the beginning of an accepted usage. In the next fifteen years, this usage evolved into a larger and more complex film syntax.

Apart from normal "punctuation marks"—fade-in/fade-out (to begin or end a scene), dissolve (for smooth transitions between shots, often indicating the passage of time), wipe, iris, and other optical effects—the core of the film "language" should be understood as having a syntactic rather than a dictionary-like nature: unlike verbal language, with its more or less fixed number of words *representing* "things," film has at its disposal a limitless vocabulary of "things" that can be seen. Out of this chaotic mass of images, the filmmaker, with either a stationary or a moving camera, captures shots selectively, framing them in a variety of graphic compositions and assigning them each a given time on the screen. The evolution of a cinema syntax made possible increasingly complex combinations of shots, which could then generate an even greater variety of messages and meanings.

In the mid-twenties, the troika of Russian filmmaker-theoreticians (Kuleshov, Vertov, and Eisenstein) acknowledged the great influence of Griffith on their filmic thinking. They, in turn, made notable contributions to advances in structural form, which then became part of the expanding film vocabulary. In this golden age of creativity, many conflicting theories and practices were put into motion.

By the late twenties, the principles of cinematic syntax were fully formulated. Such films as Eisenstein's *Potemkin* (1925), Chaplin's *The Gold Rush* (1925), Murnau's *Sunrise* (1927), Dreyer's *Passion of Joan of Arc* (1928), Pabst's *Love of Jeanne Ney* (1927), Abraham Room's *Bed and Sofa* (1927)—to mention only a few—contain most of the basic elements of syntactic conformations: specific practices for grouping shots sequentially into elements of structure and into larger units of harmony.

Most important of all was the way cinematic syntax helped define cinema as a new form of expression. At this early stage of its evolution, "cinema language" not only improved its communicative capacities but also evolved characteristic aesthetic forms which heightened that capacity. Of course, not all filmmakers chose to use those forms: through a combination of ignorance, underestimation of audience intelligence, and the need to cater to the axiomatic "lowest common denominator," sub-cinematic, nongrammatical films continued to exist, as they do today, although in most cases now they mix nonsyntactic and syntactic forms. The principal aim of such pop films was and is to deliver an entertaining narrative in a direct and quite naturalistic way.

The artists who applied the cinematic syntax, on the other hand, did not depend exclusively upon easily decipherable information to carry their narrative messages, for it is in the nature of the cinematic syntax properly used that *combinations of shots* convey far greater meaning than the sum total of the raw information contained in each shot. Such combinations touch on the mystique of cinema: a peculiar and original *cinema reality,* different from the simple mirroring of reality on the screen.

Aspects of "reality" in relation to cinema will be central to most of the theoretical considerations that follow. Let us consider first, therefore, whether the development of cinematic syntax affected the relationship between screen material and the real world. Did the fragmentation into shots, which brought about the need for grammatical order, change that relationship?

As we have seen, the early film just beginning to free itself from the theatrical tradition employed a simple "grammar" of shots arranged mainly for dramatic emphasis. Through shot distribution, the director-dramatist could control the attention of the audience by directing its gaze. While the guiding principle was dramatic emphasis, the early "grammatical" rule called for the orderly placement of shots in an identified, well-defined, and eventually familiar realistic setting. The sequence had to make clear the geography of this setting and reveal the plot in an easily comprehensible linear pattern. As in the theater-like proscenium photography, the first simple "grammar" of shots was not to tamper unduly with reality.

But fragmentation into shots is in itself a tampering with reality. To present only a realistic part of an unknown whole which the audience assumes exists outside the frame is tampering with the "wide-angle" reality by introducing assumptions instead of facts (the "things" that exist outside the limits of the picture). In a Griffith one-reeler, *Swords and Hearts* (1911), the protagonist, Ben (medium shot) is shown looking to the left, at something off screen. From previous plot information we know that he might be seeing either the girl or his horse; until the next shot gives us the answer, we cannot be sure. As it turns out, Ben sees the horse. The audience, meanwhile, has been faced with an interpretive choice, each possibility having a different dramatic meaning: what does Ben want to find first, the horse or the girl? A wide-angle "proscenium" view would not have allowed for such alternatives, because the audience would have seen Ben and the horse in the same frame.

This Griffith scene is an example of shot fragmentation in cinema which after later refinements became a structural model for conveying surprise or ambiguity by delayed disclosure. It was also a precursor of the element of separation. The grammatical rule for such fragmentation is simple: Shot 1 is a narrow fragmentation (medium shot or closer) of a "protagonist" looking toward something out of the frame; shot 2 shows (in fragmentation) what he has been looking at. Note that the order of the shots cannot be reversed without a change in the inflection or meaning.

Take another example, a western. Shot 1 is a medium shot of a cowboy shooting his gun to screen right; in shot 2 (medium close-up) the bad guy facing screen left is hit by a bullet. This is a linear action-reaction through fragmentation. Reversing the order of the shots makes the sequence nonlinear: no. 1, bad guy hit by bullet (by whom?); no. 2 cowboy with *smoking* gun (resolution). If the latter should be followed by a shot 3 of the bad guy being hit again, as an end of the "sentence," the audience would assume that the cowboy shot him again without actually seeing who did it.

Let's examine the grammatical implications of our three different examples. In the case of Ben, who may be looking for a girl or a horse, the ambiguity lies in shot 1 (Ben looking); shot 2 (the horse) partially resolves the issue. Reversing the order of shots would have completely changed the nature of the sequence. Having the horse as shot 1 would have given the answer before the question, because we would have assumed that Ben had found the horse. Ben as shot 2 would have had to make *immediate* eye contact with the horse to act out his discovery. A possible shot 3 in such a structure might have been a wider shot, showing Ben approaching the horse.

The nonlinear combination in the case of the cowboy and the bad guy is most mysterious. Seeing the bad guy is ambiguous: who shot him and why? shot 2 (cowboy with gun) is a resolution. Again, a suggested shot 3 (bad guy hit again) permits a possible "grammatical" *deletion* of the cowboy (of seeing him for the second time). In both cases, the audience must "match" shots and draw conclusions, as opposed to watching an open-frame proscenium. While there could be many variants on the above scenes, depending on the situation, plainly a proper grammatical order is always needed when assumptions, choices, and resolutions enter the process.

Film "phrases" constructed through fragmentation also tamper with reality by not showing the total geography of a setting and, more importantly, by not showing the real space or spatial relationship *between shots*, which must be assumed to exist. This manipulation of space outside the limits of a given "screen frame" becomes an important tool in structuring cinema "sentences." It permits the filmmaker to disregard *descriptive reality*. People enter and exit "frames." In continuity, an entry may be into a "frame" either geographically proximate to or far removed from the one just exited. An actor may leave a frame "now" and enter the next one days or years "later," or even, through a flashback, "before."

A less obvious and more extraordinary feature of the space outside the frame is that it can play with what is within the frame in a most dramatic fashion. It may contain the scenery or setting which the viewer imagines to be outside the limits of the screen, or it may hold a stored afterimage of a "significant form," like the figure of the Indian Chief Scarface in John Ford's *The Searchers*, which is expected to reappear at any moment on the screen. During a succession of close-ups of Actor A talking to Actor B in alternation, the viewer, as in separation, unconsciously plays the part of A while B is on the screen, and vice versa.

A film sequence generates all these effects by the use of proper syntax. The filmmaker's attention to the composing of that syntax is far more important than his meticulousness with the existing factors of the reality he is filming. In Truffaut's *Small Change* (1976), for example, there is a scene of approximately 14 shots which shows a group of young children running through narrow streets on their way home from school. In filming the scene, Truffaut used local children as his actors and a *real* school in a small town in southern France for his location. He was later criticized by the same children because, as they said, the streets in the film are not the real ones leading from the school to the village and the sequence of their running is all wrong. For those children, natives of that small town, the scene is a travesty of reality. For the viewer unfamiliar with the town, however, it is an excellent rendition of a group of kids, free and happy after the drudgery of a day in school, running downhill through the narrow streets of a charming small town. Truffaut imbued the scene with lyricism and warmth, not by following literally the "real" streets which lead from school to town, but by selecting *shots*—camera positions and locations—to conform with a plan which conveyed the essence of the situation. This involved graphic juxtapositions, symmetry, repetition, acceleration of rhythm, changes in the size of the subject, camera multiangularity, and overall harmony. Through his many directorial decisions, Truffaut created a cinema reality more effective than a mirror of the real.

So far, our examples have indicated that fragmented scenes arranged grammatically take certain liberties with reality. They have all contained straight cuts from shot to shot. By examining a longer scene with camera movement and no cuts, we may glimpse another structural element— slow disclosure. In Abraham Room's film *The Ghost that Never Returns* (1929) there is a scene which begins with an extreme close-up of a man's face. After holding for a few seconds, the camera starts a slow pullback, and as the pullback continues more and more "information" is disclosed. The initial close-up, receding and losing its intensity, starts to merge with the viewer's growing understanding of the man's sur- roundings. As the camera continues pulling farther and farther back, it goes through iron bars. At the end of the pullback, we discover that our man is actually in jail. The initial close-up of the man's face represented one reality—a man's face: the final shot, a completely different one—a man in jail. As the slow disclosure altered the reality, the scene's mean- ing changed.

Slow disclosure is singular in its intensity of effect, and not surpris- ingly it became an important element of film structure. It comes in dif- ferent gradations of impact from mild to strong and there are precise grammatical rules for its application (see chapter 7). The twisting of real- ity that takes place in the scene from Room's film shows again how the use of a syntax allows cinema to walk a tightrope between reality and illusion. Had Room not used slow disclosure and started instead with a long shot of the jail and tracked slowly through the bars into a close-up of the man's face, the scene's superficial content would have been the same, but its cinesthetic impact would have been lost.

Whenever a syntactic order is established, there is an immediate de- parture from strictly naturalistic presentation. The same is true of scenes which use elongations or condensations of real time, leaving the viewer with the intuitive "feel" of screen time which is often quite different from measurable real time. I refer not only to the visual film devices of flashback and flashforward, or to condensation through the deletion of action, but also to the ways of manipulating screen time. This usually depends upon:

(1) the size of the picture; close-ups seem to last relatively longer on the screen than long shots. The content of a close-up is immediately identified and understood. The long shot, on the other hand, is usually filled with detailed information which requires eye-scanning over the whole "tableau." The latter takes time to do, thus robbing the long shot of its screen time. The same is true of "difficult images," unusual camera angles, and unknown or unfamiliar things, all of which require time and

effort to decipher. Like the close-up, familiar images and repetitions do not need to be figured out; consequently, they seem to "linger" on the screen.

(2) the focal length of the lens used in cinematography. Movement toward and away from the camera is quite fast with wide-angle lenses and, conversely, very slow with long lenses, as in shots of people walking or cars driving endlessly toward the camera but never arriving (so popular in some recent films). Similar distortions of screen time occur through "fast motion" and, even more so, "slow motion" photography accomplished mechanically through changes in camera speed. (I consider these to be stylistic devices rather than grammatical arrangements, however, because they are used as "effects" and seldom structured into a sequence.)*

An improperly built scene cannot take the same liberties with reality that a grammatically structured scene can. In the new version of *King Kong* (1976), for example, the action near the end takes place on top of the World Trade Center in New York City. Kong, under attack by armored helicopters, is wounded and bleeding heavily; the protagonist (Jessica Lange) is also on the roof, trying desperately to help him. Eventually Kong is mortally machinegunned and falls from the skyscraper's 110th story to the street below. After two short shots of crowds, Jessica Lange appears on the street and approaches the dying colossus.

A small incident in the theater where I saw this movie may be characteristic of the audience's perception of reality. After the above scene, a little girl of seven or eight cried out loudly, "How did she [Jessica Lange] get there so fast?" Her question was reasonable. The ape fell from the roof of one of the tallest buildings in the world. How could the woman who had been beside him get to the street so fast? The film tried to condense time by deletion of action. That is a normal procedure, but one which requires the proper ordering of shots. Such an order was absent from the King Kong sequence. The rationale of the filmmaker must have been to use the two long shots of crowds converging on the dying ape as "action fillers" to give Lange "time" to come down from the 110th story. But this came after a naturalistic bloody fight scene on the roof for which minute fragmentation with close-ups was used to accommodate the needs of trick photography. Long shots after a cluster of close-ups have the function of releasing tension or of telegraphing the

---

*Jean-Luc Godard's *Every Man for Himself* (1980) is a unique exception, since the stop-slow motion is its basic element of structure.

end of a sequence. They are not useful as a device for condensing time or deleting action. As a result of this inadequacy, Lange's sudden appearance on the street is unacceptable. Under the circumstances, the only move the filmmaker could have made to satisfy the viewer's apprehension was to have a shot of the actress coming down in an elevator. Then her appearance on the street would have been more believable.

Film grammar not only affects reality on the screen, it also alters the physical reaction of the audience. A classic example is the filming of a tennis or a ping pong game. In reality, or in a proscenium presentation of such a game, the audience would be turning their heads or eyes from side to side following the rhythmical passage of the ball. In separation the head movements of the audience in the stadium would stop as if arrested, even though the rhythm of the game would continue in the same pendulum-like fashion. Interestingly enough, the rule for such an arrangement (separation) requires that occasionally an audience be shown on the screen. In turning their heads from side to side they would "release" the real audience in the movie theatre from having to do so. The whole scene could safely exist without a single overview (wide-angle shot) showing both players and spectators together on the screen. Such is the structure of the magnificent tournament scene in Bresson's *Lancelot du lac* (1975), or the tennis sequence in Hitchcock's *Strangers on a Train* (1951).

Another striking example of tampering with reality is the arrangement of "opposite movements," which is part of the element of multiangularity. Dziga Vertov developed and perfected it in the film *A Man with a Movie Camera* (1928). He found that the best way to convey the essence of a speeding automobile racing from point A to point B is to break the scene up into shots in which the car speeds in diagonally *opposite* directions, at the same time retaining a sense of the original destination (which was from A leftward to B).

The principal rule of such an arrangement is this: In shot 1, the car speeds to the left (from A); in shots 2, 3, 4, and 5 the car speeds in diagonally opposite directions (left, right, left, right), in different picture sizes, from high or low camera positions, with rhythm variations; in shot 6 (the last in the phrase), the car arrives at B from the right. The use of opposite movements does not confuse the audience about the direction of the vehicle if this rule is adhered to (even in a case where the route from A to B is geographically unfamiliar).

Ever since Vertov's experiments, opposite movements have been used in every well-constructed film where moving vehicles, or any other moving bodies, are part of the plot. Curiously enough, some directors are still cautious about it, and even though they fragment their chase scenes, they safeguard the oneness of direction, thereby abandoning the excitement inherent in opposite movements.

The move toward films which were a mosaic of fragments resulted in the development of yet another rule, according to which a wide shot, which normally conveys the most information, functions after a sequence of tighter shots as a dramatic release, rather than being solely informational. Thus, an overview shot is frequently used to end a phrase, rather than as a point of departure for a subsequent phrase. Such is the use of long shots in Murnau's *Sunrise* (1927) in the lake scenes, in the battle on the ice in Eisenstein's *Alexander Nevsky* (1938), in Hitchcock's spectacular final high long shot of the burning gas station in *The Birds* (1963), and in many other films.

Conversely, a long shot when used as the starting point for a scene and subsequently broken into details leads to a directness reminiscent of the simple grammar of the early films. This is the technique of the master shot discipline, the standard Hollywood method practiced widely since the advent of sound. According to the rules for this structure, shots 2, 3, 4, etc. are fragments from this master long shot in "magnification"—i.e., medium and close shots; at the end of the phrase comes a required return to the initial long shot (1). Most of the cuts are "invisible" in order to make the transitions smooth and to distract from the existence of cuts. Often they are on the same axis and come on movement: an actor raises a cup of coffee in long shot; the cup reaches his mouth in close-up. If dialogue is called for, it takes place, in most cases, in the classical "over the shoulder" two shots. The required return to the long shot (1), may occur several times during the scene, especially if it is of long duration.

While relatively naturalistic, the master shot technique has a definite order and its own proper "syntax." Especially after the introduction of sound, it generated increasingly realistic tendencies in film. In a grammatical context, sound dialogue forced real time upon the screen, since it takes the same time for a sentence to be uttered on the screen as it does in real life. Sound-film plot structures tended to rely more on audio than on visual information. Such masters as Lang, Renoir, Hitchcock, and Bergman have nevertheless proved that the creative use of cinesthetic elements can successfully solve the problems of handling dialogue.

From a historical perspective, it seems clear that the advent of sound was less of a barbarous shock to the art of cinema than has been commonly believed. Indeed, one can argue that film was never totally silent, but was only "deprived" of sound. In silent cinema, actors mouthed words with or without the help of title cards. "Sound-provoking" images substituted for sound effects (the barking dogs in Flaherty's *Nanook of the North* (1920) is a good example), and there was always music. Filmmakers, by necessity, used a minimum of dialogue and favored visual modes of expression. Characteristically, a fully formulated cinema syntax was in existence before the time sound was feasible.

After some hesitation while adapting to the new sound techniques in the early 1930s, progress in the evolution of "cinema language" continued. More and more complex shot configurations were introduced and new dramatic possibilities opened up. This was especially true with the use of sophisticated camera movements in combination with a cinematic mise-en-scène. The latter involved a manipulation of foreground and background action (participants moving toward or away from the camera) which created internal rhythmic pulsations in shots of long duration, the syntactic equivalent of combining shorter shots. Each new cinematic form of expression introduced different rules to assure that the shots would fall into proper place and produce a semblance of the real world. Cinematic syntax has a built-in duality: it permits the taking of liberties with a naturalistic rendition of the world, while it creates order among the shots so that they form a believable screen illusion of reality.

Theoretically, taking liberties with reality suggests a reexamination of the concept of the one-to-one ratio of picture content to meaning, for even when isolated shots carry a density of meaning, this is hinged on the shots that precede or follow. Purely independent, or one-to-one, meaning occurs only when a shot carries strong cultural associations, as does the cross or the flag. Otherwise, shots by themselves contain only surface information. The function of the cinematic syntax is to liberate the energies within that surface by creating combinations of shots which generate deeper meaning.

According to the rules of this syntax, a good film "phrase" contains a minimum of *three shots.* Two shots hint at and create expectations about the development of narrative; the third well-chosen shot will resolve those expectations. For example, if we see a medium shot of man A looking, followed by a close-up of man B, also looking, the men may—or may not—be looking at each other. If the third shot is of man A again, then the film phrase most definitely says that man A and man B are looking at each other. On the other hand, a third shot showing a close-up of a grandfather clock tells us that A and B are looking at the clock. The two alternatives illustrate the potential ambiguities of pictorial arrangement. Two pictures can tell many possible stories, and the addition of a third is necessary to complete the film statement.

The musicality and poetry of a shot sequence also seem to require a threesome, which lends a phrase a sort of melodic wholeness. This is one suggestion of the parallels between cinematic elements and the musical elements of tonality, harmony, and rhythm. Tonality, for example, is a musical convention requiring that a piece normally open and close in the same key. This parallels the symmetries in cinema, as in the first and last shots in the scene from *The Birds* (chapter 1). Similarly, the interlacing of the twelve-tone scale in harmony parallels the integration of cinesthetic elements, while the cinematic rule of a minimal unit of three parallels the accents of musical rhythm (Scriabin's tri-tone). A good example of this is the three-shot "drumbeat" in the scene from *The Birds* described in chapter 1. To satisfy narrative needs, as well as to dramatize this climax, an alternative to the three shots in *The Birds* could have been a zoom from the body of the dead farmer into his bloody face. This would have been effective (it was used in *Godfather I*) and to the point; yet the choice of a three-shot "salvo" provides a challenging phrasing at once poetic and musical. The three-shot sequence not only fulfilled the demands of narrative, but expressed itself *for* itself (as is often said of music) as well. Such is the creative application of cinematic syntax.

In a nongrammatical film, information and meaning are synonymous and remain on the surface. For example, a close-up (the overuse of which is evidence of directorial weakness and lack of structure) will most likely be used in such a film each time there is a need for strong dramatic emphasis. In a well constructed film, the shot having dramatic emphasis might be a medium, reverse angle, or moving camera shot, rather than the strongest gun in the film arsenal, the close-up. Again, only the right combination of shots yields the deeper meaning.

There is a fallacy in the assignment of fixed meaning to certain camera angles or graphic compositions. An example is the belief that exaggerated low-camera or short-focal-length-lens distortions help communicate fear or suspense. This may work on a simplistic level: reactions to fearsome pictures are easy to attain. But this is a psychic rather than a cinematic phenomenon. The reality of vivid horror, especially when presented naturalistically, will always arouse strong emotions. *Wages of Fear* by Clouzot (1953) and *Psycho* by Hitchcock (1960), on the other hand, both have many fear-provoking scenes, but they do not rely on gory images in low camera angles or short lens distortion. In a grammatical order, low camera angle is usually paired in rhythmic succession with high camera, but such an arrangement by itself does not convey any particular mood. To create a sense of fear or suspense, the filmmaker manipulates structures of content and form, selectively withholding information and creating expectations to arouse various, sometimes contradictory, assumptions in the viewer; in short, delaying the final resolution. Skillful use of cinesthetic elements accomplishes this with artistry, the harmonies of the elements bringing forth the potentialities of cinema and expressing the full meaning of a given dramatic moment (providing, of course, that the film in question has something meaningful to say).

Cinema "syntax," like the syntax of language, is in itself a *creative force*, to use Noam Chomsky's terminology. Its rules, no matter what is being expressed, make possible the formation of a large number of film phrases, including ones that have never been used before. As long as the grammatical order is adhered to, those phrases will be accepted and understood. This understanding goes beyond the ability to figure out plot intricacies, although that may be the ultimate goal. As has already been pointed out, simple communication in film can be achieved without a grammatical order, but in such cases the process of absorbing information is more or less *voyeurish*. Conversely, when a proper cinema "syntax" is used, the viewer is engaged in an active process of constantly *"matching"* chains of shots not merely by association or logical relationship but by an empathy peculiar to cinema. The blend so achieved spells cinema sense—a mixture of emotion and understanding, meditative or subliminal, engaging the viewer's ability to respond to a structured cinema "language."

Cinema "syntax," then, is an *active force* requiring audience participation. The intensity of viewer involvement depends on the energies which radiate from the screen according to the filmmaker's arrangement of dramatic trigger-release, or peak-valley sequences. When the quality of those structures is of a high order, the cumulative result is cinesthetic impact. This reinforces the proposition that most aspects of cinema are interwoven with aesthetic considerations. The masterpieces of cinema show a converging pattern wherein the artist presenting his views on life was unsatisfied with the simplistic methods of communication (so easily available in film) and so needed, and eventually developed, a "syntax" which became an excellent tool for expressing ideas and truths.

Unfortunately, the majority of films, the mediocre works, use these tools only sparingly. They arrive at meaning by mirroring a given reality, which can be lifted to significance only by borrowing the methods of the theater, the novel, and the plastic arts. Leaning on the crutch of a mixture of derivative material, the film emerges a poor imitator. Quite often it merely popularizes a work of art which has already established its reputation. Such films, in striving to communicate vibrantly, contain sequences of shots, but their shot placement and distribution are in direct service only to plot requirements and disregard the full potential of syntactic arrangement. Even though such a film is broken into shots, their order does not require participatory matching, and in many instances they could be changed with little effect, substituting close-ups for the medium or long shots, say, or unscrambling shot sequences. This is a sure indicator that there is no need for a "due arrangement of shots to show their mutual relation in a sequence," as there would be in a syntactically constructed film.

The cinesthetic structures cannot exist without a meticulous order which, like language, has a built-in capacity for innumerable variants. To reiterate, a cinematic syntax yields meaning not only through the surface content of shots but also through their connections and mutual relationships. Ambiguities can be achieved by using specific combinations, thus providing the concrete image with some of the ambivalence of the word. Examples to support this notion can be found in the aforementioned scene from Griffith and in the imaginary scene of man A and man B looking at each other or at a clock. A still more telling example is found in a recurring scene in Alain Resnais's *Providence* (1976). It takes place in a morgue, where a doctor performs an autopsy on an old man's cadaver. The vividness of this action—his scalpel opening chest and stomach—after two repetitions acquires new dimensions, but remains ambiguous. The scene is not directly connected with the plot of the film, yet it is not puzzling, and it never loses its shocking reality. In the context of the film, which deals principally with old age and death, this semi-abstract scene stops being what it really is (while *remaining* a vivid action). This may sound like a paradox, but the integration Resnais achieved by using this familiar image imbues it with a kind of cinematic "thought." It retains its ambivalence without suggesting literary symbolism.

Needless to say, there is a world of difference between language and cinema. To paraphrase Nietzsche, words do not designate things, are not little labels stuck on things, but are "an army of metaphors" for real things in the world.* In the early days, filmmakers, including Eisenstein, attempted pictorial metaphor and simile. Since then, however, literary metaphor has almost disappeared from the film vocabulary. Things on the screen do not reach us via words but via experience.

Words make no sense unless they are in grammatical order, and even so arranged they often lose their connection with the concreteness of life. In cinema, pictures never lose contact with life. The binding arrangement of words does not exist in cinema, because the conjunctions of shots are open-ended.

Yet, a distinction must still be made between the nonmetaphoric nature of filmic imagery (which is lifelike) and a nonmetaphoric *order* of images. The former leaves impressions while the latter generates expression. Order implies syntax, and it is this syntax which is a source of significantly expressive cinema.

Cinema "syntax" creates a *nonmetaphoric order of things;* the result is an intellectual and aesthetic experience quite different from the one we are accustomed to in our language-dominated culture. Perhaps in the future, cinema art will perfect this nonmetaphoric order and attain that closeness to the "true" which language by nature can never attain.

In this chapter I have attempted to introduce the general idea of a cinematic syntax. It is difficult to argue convincingly for syntax in a medium which can operate with great popular success using only vestiges of such an order, even though it often limps along on the fringe of cinematic illiteracy as a result. In any case, the dichotomy between the "easy" film and the "complex" cinema becomes clearer. Like other arts, cinema may have to suffer lesser popularity if it is to gain the eventual distinction of serving truly humanistic goals.

In the chapters ahead I shall return to the practical matter of spelling out the rules of syntactic order, but first I shall comment on the creative process with a focus on the master plan as the important step in preparing a work of cinema.

* Friedrich Nietzsche, *Werke* (Berlin: Collin, 1973).

3

The Master Plan

THE intrinsic nature of a cinematic syntax must be reconciled with the persistent dependence of the film medium on literature and the theater, which continue to exert considerable influence on the creative process of filmmaking. This influence, which often conflicts with the structural requirements of cinema, becomes apparent in the initial stages of creation, the preparation of a screenplay.

I do not intend to discuss here the techniques of screenwriting and its related practices (a script is often used as a "presentation" for producers' approval, for obtaining financial backing, attracting actors, etc.). What I would like to stress is that the screenplay as the plan for a future film is usually a literary conception, suited to the verbal mode. Thus the mental process of creating a film begins to be channeled into a different realm—that of literature and theater. Consequently, the filmmaker later finds himself *translating* this literary material into a set of provocative images to suit the need and flavor of the written story.

But filmic images in a chain, no matter what their content or graphic composition, do not inherently express designated moods or emotional states. The desired effect is conditioned by the *continuous flow* of pictures, and, to be fully meaningful, can be produced only through a structure-dependent sequence. This dependence on structure is as vital to the art of cinema as grammatical order is to verbal language. In sum, screen imagery is not conducive to *direct* translation, although adaptations are possible.

Potentially, literature and cinema are both story-telling mediums requiring good stories "adapted" to their respective means of expression. Happily, life in the world around us is full of material for films, books, painting, music, and poetry to draw on; so there is no reason why film should depend so heavily on literary sources. The "cinematic" quality of some books is a gross misconception; for cinema *shows* a story with methods totally different from those a book uses, regardless of how action-filled or image-provoking the text is. Even though dialogue is crucial to the story, cinema operates in a visual mode: there are always images on the screen. Dialogue, with its potential for beauty and meaning, is really another one of the "things" of reality to be ordered in a film; in the context of cinema's total structure, it stands as one of many elements. Yet a well-written script uses the conceptualizations of another matrix—the literary. The narrative, to be readable, is "visualized" according to literary stimuli. This image-provoking through words plainly differs from pure visual imagery and visual thinking.

Ideally, cinematic treatment should start with a central mythos—the essence of what is to be conveyed. Such a brief statement of purpose would then be followed by an outline of actual events, including dialogue and a cinematic structural continuity. The final master plan would be a mixture of architectural blueprint, symphonic score, battle strategy, and choreographic composition with signs, symbols, sketches, and notes: rather an unreadable affair.*

The cinema artist, like all artists, has something to say about his human interests and experience, and this creative urge takes both abstract and concrete forms. He needs to think of elements in cinema which correspond to the abstract/concrete complex taking shape in his mind in order to express his idea in a way that defines it. This cannot be accomplished by translating an existing literary script into a set of approximate visual correlatives. In order to express his ideas the filmmaker must draw from the internal resources of cinema.

The previous chapters have discussed the existence and potential of a cinematic syntax and its structure; the same arguments now lead to a recognition of the importance to cinema of a master plan, the formulation of which necessarily precedes the building of a new work. In cinema, as in the other arts, the question of *what* to do converges with that of *how* and by *what means* to do it (material, style, genre etc.).

A master plan is vital to cinema for reasons peculiar to the medium, including the largeness of its "canvas," the complexity of its technical

*Cinema will eventually develop a uniform system of notations like those in music and dance (Labannotations) which will show the orchestrated cinesthetic "score" of the proposed work.

base, and most importantly, the newness of its elements. The nature of cinema, as discussed in the previous chapters, suggests that the narrative elements contained in the master plan should be generated by the structure of cinema's syntax.

A good example of such a narrative is the well-known scene on the Odessa Steps in Eisenstein's *Potemkin* (1925). To illustrate, a shot-by-shot breakdown of the final part of this scene follows. It is 75 seconds long and contains 55 shots (see analysis pp. 41–52).

This scene is a model for a structure-generated narrative. Thematically, it comprises a few simple components:

1. The Odessa Steps
2. The attacking soldiers, running people and people wounded or dead

Table 3.1. Shot Topics

Shot Numbers							
1–7	Soldiers	Mother and Baby	Soldiers	Mother's Face	Baby	Mother and Baby	Mother's Face
8–14	Soldiers Fire	Mother Shot-Face	Buggy Wheels	Mother's Face	Mother's Tummy	Crowd	Mother's Tummy
15–21	Mother's Tummy	Mother's Face	Mother and Baby	Buggy Wheels	Soldiers	Soldiers	Mother and Buggy
22–28	Buggy Wheels	Crowd	Crowd	Crowd	Mother and Buggy	Buggy Descends Stairs	Mother and Buggy
29–35	Elderly Woman	Buggy	Crowd and Buggy	Crowd and Buggy	Crowd	Dead Mother	Buggy
36–43	Elderly Woman	Buggy	Student	Crowd	Buggy	Student	Buggy
43–49	Baby	Buggy	Baby	Soldiers	Student	Buggy	Buggy
50–55	Buggy	Student	Buggy Tips	Soldiers	Soldier	Elderly Woman	Fade Out

3. Mother with baby in carriage: the baby in carriage is the "protagonist" of the story
4. Woman with pince-nez: a significant image of great pathos which ends the sequence (three shots)
5. Student-spectator: a thread connecting and paralleling the carriage's fall (four shots)

Most of the shots are rotated as familiar images, becoming elements of separation and parallel actions, and are structured in a variation on multiangularity known as Eisensteinian "clashing shots." The scene ends in a beat of three close-ups: two of the soldiers wielding sabers, and the final familiar image of the woman with pince-nez, her glasses shattered—fade-out.

If we divide the scene into three "cadenzas" (see Table 3.2), an ingenious placement of shots becomes evident. In the first cadenza of 11 shots, the mother is most prominent. In the second cadenza, in which she is killed, there are 3 shots of her. In the third cadenza, she is absent;

Table 3.2. Distribution of Shots According to Topic

	Shots 1–18	Shots 19–36	Shots 37–55
Soldiers	3	2	3
Mother	11	3	0
Carriage	6	9	10
Crowd	1	6	1
Spectators	0	2	5

Table 3.3 Distribution of Shot Types

	Shots 1–18	Shots 19–36	Shots 37–55
Extreme close-up through medium close-up	10	5	14
medium through long	7	7	4
extra-long	1	6	1

Table 3.4. Distribution of Shots According to Angle

	Shots 1–18	Shots 19–36	Shots 37–55
high angle	4	8	11
eye level	9	5	4
low angle	5	5	3

THE ODESSA STEPS

Shot 1. 27 frames, 1.12 seconds. Low-angle medium shot. Soldiers, with their guns, march from left to right. They are shown from knees to chest. Their black pants and guns stand out against the white sky.

Shot 2. 92 frames, 3.83 seconds. Medium long shot. The mother and her baby carriage are shown for the first time. She rushes to the center of the frame, stops, and looks around. People are rushing by her right to left. The mother is trying to protect her baby and is caught in the crowd. Dressed in black, the mother stands out against the white sky and pale buildings of the city below.

Shot 3. 44 frames, 1.83 seconds. Long shot: The soldiers march left to right down the steps with their guns. The shot begins with the soldiers already in the frame and ends before they leave the frame. In this shot, the soldiers' white jackets serve to distinguish them from the dark trees in the background. The direction of their movement is the same as shot 1 and opposite to that in shot 2. Their shadows fall behind them.

Shot 4. 39 frames, 1.62 seconds. Close up: the mother, her mouth open at the start of the shot. She closes it and then opens it again as she looks in terror at the soldiers. She is in the center, a strong black image against a white background.

Shot 5. 42 frames, 1.75 seconds. Medium close-up. Baby in the carriage. We see the mother's scarf and her hand as it moves left to right along the side of the carriage. In the background, people run left to right.

Shot 6. 35 frames, 1.45 seconds. Medium long shot. Mother standing between carriage and foreground. Shot starts with man passing between mother and the camera; picked up mid-frame, he proceeds from right to left until he leaves the frame. Others rush right to left behind her and one runs in front of her gaze. The town is visible in the background. The mother, in the center of the frame, bends over and looks to the left at the soldiers (same composition as in shot 2).

Shot 7. 19 frames, .79 second. Close-up of the mother. The same composition as shot 4. The mother is centered in this eye-level shot and her face stands out against her black clothing, a bold image against the light sky. She first looks left (as in the previous shot), and then slightly to the right. She opens her mouth and screams. She then moves her head left slightly before looking farther right with her mouth still open.

Shot 8. 19 frames, .79 second. Low-angle medium shot. The soldiers are firing their guns, smoke curling from the gun tips. The black guns stand out against the light sky. As we watch the soldiers from their knees to their guns, we see four layers of contrast: black pants, white jackets, black guns, and white sky.

Shot 9. 42 frames, 1.75 seconds. Close-up. Mother's face. She is hit. She is center frame with her eyes half closed. She opens her mouth and moves left and back. Her eyes roll up until only the whites are visible. Her head continues moving until we see under her chin and up her nose. The background is out of focus. The composition is similar to that of shots 4 and 7, except that this shot is low angle. A strong image with the face pale, scarf dark, background light.

Shot 10. 30 frames, 1.25 seconds. High-angle, close-up. The carriage wheels start to go over the step and then pull back, moving right to left and back again. We also observe the shadows of the wheels on the three steps. The shadows fall in front of the carriage, unlike the shadows of the soldiers.

Shot 11. 51 frames, 2.12 seconds. Low-angle close-up. The mother as she continues to move from her position in shot 9. Her head is back, as it was in shot 9, and she moves it left to right. She opens her eyes, looks up with her mouth open. The composition is the same as shot 9.

Shot 12. 83 frames, 3.45 seconds. Close-up. Her white-gloved hands move downward from the top of the frame, and clutch her stomach where she has presumably been shot. Her belt buckle is centered in the frame.

Shot 13. 69 frames, 2.86 seconds. Extreme long shot. The people descending the steps, from the top of the screen to the bottom in a direct and diagonal manner. Soldiers on horses are situated at the bottom of the steps, trying to prevent the crowd's escape.

Shot 14. 46 frames, 1.92 seconds. Close-up. Mother's belly and white-gloved hands. As she squeezes, blood covers her gloves and her belt buckle. As in shot 12, her white-gloved hands provide a strong image against black clothing and blood. Her hands move slightly in a clasping manner. The blood is immediately evident on the white gloves.

Shot 15. 20 frames, .85 seconds. Medium shot. Still holding her stomach, the mother moves down and slightly back. A small portion of the carriage is visible behind her.

Shot 16. 87 frames, 3.63 seconds. Extreme close-up. The mother's face. At the beginning of the shot, part of her head is shown in the frame, but no facial features can be seen. As she moves right to left into the center of the frame, her eyes look to the right and slightly upward, with a pained look. She closes her eyes and sinks out of the frame until only the white background remains.

Shot 17. 93 frames, 3.87 seconds.
A. Medium shot. Clutching her stomach, the mother continues falling. She sinks down into the frame, below the carriage handle, and out of frame. She stares straight ahead. In the background, people are running right to left behind the carriage. As the mother falls, the baby and carriage are revealed behind her. The mother's head vanishes in the lower left corner of the frame. The town is visible in the background.

B. Medium shot. The mother out of frame, we see the baby crying and reaching for his mother. The focal point is the baby. The people keep running behind the carriage, right to left. Finally, the carriage starts to move left.

Shot 18. 28 frames, 1.17 seconds. Close-up. This shot has the same composition as shot 10. The wheels of the carriage move right to left on the first of the three steps pictured. The wheels then move back again. They still don't go over the step. The shadows from the wheels fall in front of the carriage on the step below.

Shot 19. 30 frames, 1.25 seconds. Medium shot. Soldiers descend the steps left to right, opposite in direction to the previous shot. We see them from boots to thighs. At the beginning of the shot, the legs are in the center of the frame. After the legs march right and leave the frame, we see only the stairs and the soldiers' shadows left behind them. The image of black vertical legs moving against horizontal steps is very effective.

Shot 20. 32 frames, 1.33 seconds. Low-angle, medium-long shot. The soldiers march left to right. We see them from knees to guns. A few heads are also visible. Here we have two layers of darkness: black pants, white jackets, black guns, white jackets again, and white sky.

Shot 21. 52 frames, 2.17 seconds. High-angle medium shot. Starts with the mother in the center of the frame facing screen right. She first appears from chin to thigh, then falls until her face appears. Clutching her stomach, she moves right and then left, falling on the baby carriage and pushing it. The shot ends with the mother in a sitting position leaning on the carriage.

Shot 22. 13 frames, .46 seconds. High-angle close-up.
A. The carriage wheels pass over the steps for the first time. The shot starts with the wheels already in motion just left of the center of the frame. The wheels' shadows precede them onto the steps below.

B. This shot's composition is the same as that of shots 10 and 18 (the precarious carriage).

Shot 23. 12 frames, .50 seconds. Extreme long shot. The people run chaotically down the steps while the soldiers follow behind them in two lines (black filled in marks on drawing). Since this shot is only one half of a second, we have only a glance of the action. By this time, the running crowd is a familiar image.

Shot 24. 32 frames, 1.33 seconds. Extreme long shot. The Cossack horsemen block the crowd's escape at the bottom of the stairs. The crowd runs down the steps from the top of the frame, vertical figures moving down the horizontal stairs.

Shot 25. 23 frames, .96 seconds. Extreme long shot. The crowd is still running as in the two previous shots, but in this one a side view of the crowd and steps is presented. In the foreground what appears to be a doctor is helping a wounded person. Other wounded and dead are near the white-coated doctor. A fence spearates the doctor and wounded from the fleeing people.

Shot 26. 11 frames, .46 seconds. High-angle medium shot. The mother continues her falling action from where she left off in shot 21. The mother's head falls right to left, pushing the carriage wheels. At the end of the shot, the mother is in a horizontal position in contrast to her sitting position at the beginning of the shot.

Shot 27. 17 frames, .71 seconds. Close-up. The steps. The baby carriage enters in the lower right corner of the frame and proceeds left. The shot ends with the baby's face in the center of the frame. This is a cut on movement. The baby is crying.

Shot 28. 14 frames, .58 seconds. High-angle close-up. In this side view of the wheels and the mother's head, the wheel spokes and rims appear white, while the black image of the mother's head pushes on them, causing them to travel right to left at the end of the shot. The mother's face can then be clearly seen. At the end of the shot one half of a wheel is still in the frame.

Shot 29. 7 frames, .29 seconds. Low medium close-up. An elderly lady with a pince-nez has her arms raised and her mouth open as she screams. Because of the juxtaposition of this shot with the previous shot and the following shot of the carriage, we believe that she is reacting to that incident.

Shot 30. 46 frames, 1.92 seconds. Medium shot. The first traveling shot in this sequence. All of the previous shots were static. The carriage is seen as it bounces down the stairs, moving from the lower left of the frame to the lower right. The carriage is in a similar position on the screen for the duration of the shot. As it moves, it passes dead bodies. The carriage moves on a perpendicular to the lines of the stairs.

Shot 31. 38 frames, 1.58 seconds. Long shot. The carriage bounces down the steps from the upper left of the screen to the middle of the frame. In this side view of the steps, the fleeing people run from screen upper left to middle right. The carriage passes behind hanging leaves. There are trees in the background, along with bodies.

Shot 32. 72 frames, 3 seconds. Long shot. This is the second side view of the carriage descending the steps. The carriage travels from the upper left to the lower right. The people run in the same direction. Bodies are on the steps. Trees are in the background.

Shot 33. 41 frames, 1.71 seconds. Extra long shot. Cossack horsemen are pictured blocking the escape of the fleeing Odessan citizens. The crowd runs from the top of the frame down and to the sides. Horsemen stab and shoot the people. The composition of this shot is similar to that of shot 24. The vertical figures run down the horizontal steps.

Shot 34. 15 frames, .63 seconds. Medium shot. The dead mother is in a horizontal position and parallel to the steps, suggesting calm. A black figure.

Shot 35. 25 frames, 1.04 seconds. High-angle, medium shot. The carriage bounces down the stairs from left to right. Throughout the shot, the camera *travels* with the carriage down the steps and over dead bodies. The carriage's shadow travels in front of it. The carriage stays in the same position in the lower center of the frame as it moves perpendicularly to the steps. The composition of this shot is the same as that of shot 30.

Shot 36. 31 frames, 1.29 seconds. Eye level, close-up. The woman in the pince-nez (as in shot 29). She looks slightly left with her mouth open. Because of the juxtaposition of shots, we assume that she is watching the baby carriage bounce down the steps. The background is blurred.

Shot 37. 49 frames, 2.04 seconds. Medium close-up. The lower portion of the carriage. The moving wheels are situated in the center of the frame and remain there for the duration of this shot. The carriage's shadow is evident in front of it on the steps. As it bounces down the stairs, the carriage travels over dead bodies.

Shot 38. 13 frames, .54 seconds. Close-up. Apparently watching the carriage, a young man looks screen right. Next to him is a mirror. Because of the juxtaposition of the shots, we assume that this student is watching the carriage's descent.

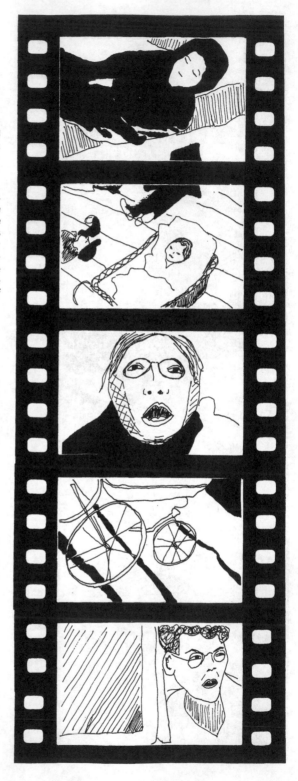

Shot 39. 56 frames, 2.33 seconds. Extra long shot. Beyond the fence, the Odessan citizens are running for their lives. In the foreground, the same doctor as in shot 25 is helping the same wounded person when a boy jumps over the fence, is shot, and falls, joining the other bodies. The composition here is the same as shot 25. The living people are perpendicular to the steps, while the dead are parallel to the steps. The white-coated doctor stands out in a field of dark bodies.

Shot 40. 28 frames, 1.17 seconds. High-angle medium shot. The camera travels overhead. The baby carriage moves from the lower left of the frame to the upper left corner until the baby's head is no longer visible. The carriage's shadow precedes the carriage on a flat landing rather than on the steps.

Shot 41. 25 frames, 1.04 seconds. Close-up. Watching the descent of the carriage, the student follows it with his eyes, right to left. A reflection of his head is evident in the mirror next to him, giving the feeling of two reactions. The composition is the same as that of shot 38.

Shot 42. 28 frames, 1.17 seconds (same as shot 37). Medium close-up. The carriage bounces down the steps, with the baby not visible, its shadow in front as the camera follows the buggy in a traveling shot. The wheels stay in center left of the frame as the carriage moves left to right.

Shot 43. 27 frames, 1.13 seconds. High-angle close-up. The baby moving from center frame to the upper left corner, where it passes out of the frame. In this traveling shot, the camera follows the baby before stopping to allow the baby's face to pass out of the frame. The shot ends with the baby's covers passing in front of the camera. Opposite direction to that of the previous shot.

Shot 44. 23 frames, .96 seconds. Medium close-up (same as shots 37 and 42). The baby carriage descends the steps left to right over dead bodies. The camera travels with the carriage, keeping it in the same screen position.

Shot 45. 10 frames, .42 seconds. Close-up. The baby stays in the center of the frame with his left hand over his left eye for the duration of the shot. As in shot 43, the baby is traveling right to left.

Shot 46. 19 frames, .79 seconds. Low-angle medium shot. Soldiers' legs and guns as they fire down on the people: dead bodies, and waving, pleading white arms and hands reaching out to the soldiers. Smoke comes from the guns. The vertical legs are a strong contrast to the horizontal steps.

Shot 47. 6 frames, .25 seconds. Close-up. The horrified student screams. He is looking screen left and presumably reacting to the situation. His reflection is seen in the mirror next to him. Shots 38 and 41 have the same composition.

Shot 48. 9 frames, .38 seconds. Medium-angle close-up. The carriage. The baby carriage is in the center, traveling from center screen out of frame. Opposite movement.

Shot 49. 17 frames, .71 seconds. Medium close-up (the same as shots 37, 42, and 44). The carriage wheels are just left of center. They pass from left to right down the stairs and over the dead bodies. Camera travels with the carriage.

Shot 50. 26 frames, 1.08 seconds. Overhead medium shot. The carriage moves from lower left to upper left corner where the baby's head goes out of frame. As in shot 40, the camera travels with the carriage on the flat pavement, rather than on the steps. Shot 40 has the same composition.

Shot 51. 7 frames, .29 second. Close-up. As in shots 38, 41, and 47, we again see the student's reflection in the mirror in the left of the frame. The student looks screen right, reacting to the baby's fate.

Shot 52. 13 frames, .54 second. Medium shot. There is a slight camera movement as the carriage tips over at the bottom of the steps. The carriage is situated in lower-center frame.

Shot 53. 6 frames, .25 second. Medium close-up. Soldier. From a low angle, we see him swing his saber toward the camera. Behind him is a brick building. This is the first shot in which a soldier is seen in close-up facing the camera.

Shot 54. 25 frames, 1.04 seconds. Low-angle close-up: Another soldier. He swings his saber toward the camera and back again several times. The same brick building as in the previous shot is in the background.

Shot 55. 43 frames, 1.79 seconds. Close-up. Blood streaming from her right eye, her glasses smashed, the elderly woman with the pince-nez, her mouth open, screams. This ends the sequence.

the focus shifts to the carriage and the baby. Views of the carriage gradually increase in frequency through the three cadenzas from 6 to 9 to 10—as do the high angles—4 to 8 to 11. Shots of the crowd and extra-long shots are symmetrically distributed—1 to 6 to 1. Close-ups have a pattern close to the formula 2-1-3 (10 to 5 to 14). The main threats in the narrative, the soldiers, have a minimal exposure, 3 to 2 to 3.

The story content of the sequence is simple, while its visual elaboration is extensive. The linearity of events, which has a distinct beginning and end, is complicated by the complex parallelism of the several actions.

Let us look at one detail—the mother's death:

Shot 7: A close-up of mother begins the sequence
Shot 8: Soldiers fire;
Shot 9: close-up of her, as She is *hit* by bullets

So far, we have three shots of linear narrative consequence. The next shot (10) introduces the motif of the baby carriage's movement. The mother's falling into death begins in the following shot (11) and continues until shot 28, interrupted ten times by brief parallel actions: soldiers, running crowd, and precarious carriage. The mother's death is spread over a span of 18 shots, including the parallel actions. This long visual elaboration on her death is typical of a structure-generated narrative. The cinematic "story" touches not only upon the pathos and tragedy of her death but also upon that of the sum of the other thematic layers involved. The scene radiates intensity to the implied actions outside the limits of the frame, creating an even larger canvas.

The Odessa scene demonstrates how an idea found definition on the screen, not via translation from a literary script, but in a combination of elements native to cinema. The same can be said of works of cinema that use structures different from Eisenstein's. Max Ophuls, in his *La Ronde* (1950), used scenes of longer duration with a moving camera. He could have used many possible techniques to adapt this stage play to the screen, but the elegant fluidity of his camera created a cinesthetic impact possible only with solutions of cinematic form. The structural elements he used were in his mind, as they were in Eisenstein's, even before the story existed, just as the structures of syntax are in a novelist's mind before he writes a single sentence.

Confronted with scenes of irreproachable artistry, we must conclude that the notion of translation must be bypassed. The same material then takes the form of a narrative without literary roots.

A literary script can truly be written only *after* a film is made. In *Frenzy* (1972), Hitchcock used only a list of 109 shots on a yellow pad for the shooting of the scene in the lorry loaded with potato bags.* In one of the bags is the body of a murdered woman, and the protagonist (the murderer) is trying to recover his tie pin, possible evidence against him, which is clutched in her dead hand. All the directorial decisions were set down precisely on paper in the form of those 109 camera instructions. A writer's concept, while giving a vivid description of the event, would not, via translation, have inspired the 109 shots. In a master plan with a cinematic structure, as in *Potemkin,* conjunctions between shots could not have been predicted by a "literary" plan. The potato bag sequence in *Frenzy* was so precisely planned (some cuts less than a second long) in concordance with the total scheme for the film that editing was a simple matter of splicing shots together.

Conversely, the "translation" method precipitates a crisis in the editing stage when the director or editor come to the conclusion that the film material does not fit well together. They go through a second process of organizing shots, perhaps different from the original script concept. This doctoring of the film in the editing stage is usually a rescue operation, not always consistent with a cinematic concept of harmony. Once the scenes are shot, they often become self-contained episodes that do not lend themselves to cinesthetic interlocking.

Arthur Penn's *Bonnie and Clyde* (1967) went through a stage of editorial doctoring and illustrates the problems which result from such procedures. The film has linear continuity—a core of realistic scenes derived directly from the story material. It is superbly acted, but the fine performances do not make up for a basic lack of structure. The connections between scenes are unplanned and the result is jumpy and disorienting to the viewer. In each scene, the viewer must correct this disorientation and reaffirm the continuity of the realistic core. Possibly single camera positions were deemed insufficient for a long stretch of acting and, as is often the practice, many camera viewpoints were filmed only as contingencies. Final decisions were then made in the editing room, as afterthoughts.

While one cannot completely dismiss the possibility of ideas occurring during or after shooting, they too must be compatible with a general scheme. The system of building a work of cinema affords many layers of control: retakes, postdubbing, final editing, music. But such

* From the author's conversations with Hitchcock, Columbia University, 1975.

adjustments, changes, and possible corrections cannot substitute for a master plan. In the period from 1924 to 1934, the editing room was indeed a laboratory for experimenting with different models of construction. Now, however, with most of the basic components of structure tested and successfully used, there is ample opportunity to shift to an all-syntactic cinema.

It is a prevailing notion that filmmaking is a collaborative effort that involves many craftspeople. Indeed, this is so—in the sense that the Sistine Chapel ceiling, a Frank Lloyd Wright design, or a giant sculpture by Jacques Lipshitz is a collaborative effort. Doubtless, creative associates help shape the director's work. Theoretically, however, it is of no import who contributes ideas for a film or to what extent they prevail, as long as an integrated master plan is formulated. The director who "calls the shots" is obviously in a central position and as an artist must be "fluent" in all the crafts of his art in order to absorb intelligently and apply creatively the contributions of others. Frank Lloyd Wright believed that an architect should know how to lay bricks as well as how to figure stresses of materials; otherwise his structures would collapse. Figuratively speaking, a film without a solid master plan can also collapse.

Knowledge of the conventions governing cinema and understanding of which combination of elements is relevant to a particular structure is a way toward cinematic originality. The filmmaker can then discover new combinations; indeed he can form new ones *ad infinitum* without adhering to a classical formula.

> The possession of originality cannot make an artist unconventional; it drives him further into convention, obeying the law of the art itself, which seeks constantly to reshape itself from its own depths, and which works through its geniuses for metamorphosis, as it works through minor talents for mutation.*

Without organic integration of the "syntactic" components—those mutations in cinema—originality is a mere trickery that degenerates into a series of effects.

We return to the assertion that cinema is a moving sequence of shots which depends on harmony and *wholeness*, not on the thrust of one interesting shot idea, a "one liner" type. One shot is *not* a cinematic unit. As original as that single shot might be in cinema angle, graphics,

---

*Northrop Frye, *Anatomy of Criticism* (Princeton: Princeton University Press, 1957), p. 132.

acting, etc., a scene depending on it alone will not work dynamically; it will instead become banal and pedestrian. Single "great shot" ideas bespeak their translation from the literary sentence's single idea.

An example of strained originality is Noel Black's film *Pretty Poison* (1968). The film's continuity equates close-ups with introspection, the examination of the mind of the main character, when close-ups in fact have no more correlation with introspection than they do with specific emotions. Although the equation close-up equals introspection sounds logical, it does not suffice on the screen. The logic of cinema is of a different nature, outside of cause and effect inevitability. Direct visual metaphors and literal interpretations—as when Eisenstein equated Kerensky with a strutting peacock in *October* (1927)—have disappeared from the screen.

In Don Siegel's *The Shootist* (1976) with John Wayne and Jimmy Stewart, there is a great shot through the spokes of a rolling wagon wheel of Wayne walking down the street of a western town. At first, the front wheels roll in close-up, and through them we see Wayne far off, crossing the street. Then the larger rear wheels come into view framing him in their motion, an original and gratifying shot. Unfortunately, this cuts directly to a "tell the story," plain, medium shot of Wayne continuing his walk. The transition, while narratively logical, is cinematicly ill-fitting, undercutting the great shot and thereby negating its meaning. Such a shot would seem promising in a script but on the screen it has no support from the structural unity of the sequence.

George Roy Hill's use of slow motion is another example of "one liner" rather than structured originality. After a shoot-out in the last scene of *Butch Cassidy and the Sundance Kid* (1969), the victims fall and hit the dirt in slow motion. A comparatively new film experience at the time, this metaphor now triggers instant recognition in an audience seeing it in another film. Certain effects, when imitated, smack of outright plagiarism. Slow motion *was* used by Kurosawa in *The Seven Samurai* (1954). Unlike Hill, Kurosawa broke up his sequence with a series of cuts, interrupting the slow motion several times with other action. He thus incorporated the effect into an overall structure. In such a combination of shots one can be truly original. The resulting cinesthetic impact is an outgrowth of harmonic structures, the sort of impact that scripted words cannot predict.

The most striking and innovative use of slow motion can be seen in Jean-Luc Godard's *Every Man for Himself* (1980). The film's singular expressiveness is keyed in repeated sequences of slow-stop motion scenes, orchestrated throughout the length of the film. The result is spectacular, thought provoking, and emotionally intense and real, yet curiously ambivalent; the best example I know of an elegant cinematic metaphor totally free of literary roots.

Roman Polanski achieves originality in *Knife in the Water* (1961) by using a series of camera *side movements* resulting in a flotation of figures and faces entering, leaving, and crossing to the other side of the frame. This movement was consistently orchestrated throughout the film. The floating images juxtaposed against the movement of the small sailing boat, where most of the action takes place, is like a ballet of graphics lending nuances and ambiguities to the interplay of characters. Polanski has said that he made extensive tests, experiments, and sketches before a master plan was established. The stylistic unity of the film *yields* the narrative information.

In the last scene of John Ford's *The Searchers* (1956) John Wayne is seen through the doorway of the ranch, walking away into the distant landscape—a group of shots brilliantly embodying the idea of a lonely figure on a desolate path. Would the meaning of this closing shot have been different if it were not composed through the frame of the doorway, a form of significance and, because of repeated use, of familiarity in the film? Alternative compositions for this scene are many—all of them potentially "pictorial equivalents" for the idea of a lonely hero going away. Ford's repeated use of the door frame as a familiar image imbues it with both dramatic and graphic significance. It introduces symmetry by repetition and creates a vertical contrast (the doorway) to the Vistavision horizontal shape of the frame. This structural design complements the story idea with a "turn of phrase" of cinematic, not verbal, conception—just as Eisenstein's choice of the form of the Odessa Steps "underlined" the horizontality of his frame, emphasizing simultaneously the brutal verticality of the attacking soldiers and the diagonal descent of the baby carriage.

To summarize, the master plan contains the "score" for a film's sequence of shots and the system for their interlocking; it is an abstraction for a future visual elaboration of a "story." The intensity of a cinema experience is governed by the artist's knowledge of cinema's means of expression and his talent and skill in using them. The master plan for a properly organized film is like a one-man game of chess in which all moves are planned in advance and all countermoves anticipated. Such cinema communicates deeper meaning through a structural "order of things" selected from the chaos of surrounding reality. And this order is basically different from the one used in organizing words to generate meaning: the two are on different intellectual and cognitive planes. There is no easy crossover from the "metaphoric" nature of words to the "nonmetaphoric order of things" of cinema. When a translation is attempted, the metaphoric language of literature is stripped naked, and what remains is but a shadow of life.

I do not mean to diminish the contribution of the talented writers who, since the advent of sound, have been responsible for the creation of meaningful dialogue in numerous films of varying quality. Yet the building blocks of film and literature are not necessarily compatible.

Fluctuations in a film's quality may well be due partially to a malaise in the initial stages of the creative process—the tendency to translate from the verbal to the visual mode. The screenplay-dominated film has not yet broken its umbilical cord to literature and theater; it still operates on a similar conceptual wavelength. A master plan which uses the known values of the cinematic "syntax" like notes in a score can, on the other hand, help create works uniquely cinematic in a predictable, meaningful, and artistic fashion. I would rather see a filmmaker with a sure concept of form in search of a story than see someone with a story in pursuit of a form. The latter is like a translator searching for the appropriate words. For in an understanding of cinematic form as I have described it lies a composite thrust, in itself a possible path, though not necessarily a shortcut, toward the large score embodied in a work of cinema. With that basic proposition in mind the following chapters will examine the eight elements of cinematic structure, starting with separation.

4

Separation

SEPARATION is an arrangement of shots showing subjects *one at a time* on the screen; i.e., a scene of two people talking to each other in separate frames in an A,B,A,B,A,B arrangement. Separation can accommodate any given thematic situation, but cinematically, its specialty lies in the ability to create intimate relationships between parts seen separately on the screen. This element of structure is a singular and superb vehicle of cinematic expression. Unparalleled in any other medium, it contains the ingredients of cinema "language" in the purest sense. There are three facets to separation, which I shall discuss in turn:

(1) the graphic and spatial composition of the images, including introduction and resolution.
(2) rhythm and apparent time: a time sense unique to separation in cinema.
(3) the "intimacy" of the relationship between the separated images.

Graphic and Spatial Composition

For the sake of clarity, I shall illustrate a hypothetical separation of two people, although this element can involve more participants. A separation usually begins with an introduction in the form of a full shot, which clearly conveys the geographical whereabouts of the participants and their spatial relationship to each other. Even with such an introduction, however, the viewer's retention of this geography is minimal, especially when a separation scene lasts for an extensive number of shots, say 15.

To begin, we shall again use the hypothetical situation of man A looking at man B in a succession of shots A,B,A,B,A,B. An important rule in separation is that of *perspectivization:* the two men are at a distance from each other and accordingly should *not* be of the same picture size on the screen. The difference in size creates the necessary sense of perspective. For instance, showing A in close-up as shot 1 (face only) and B in medium close-up as shot 2 (face plus shoulders) implies that they are a small distance apart. If shot 2 were medium shot size (head to hip) it would indicate a greater distance between them. In separation, identical size pictures don't "ring true," and one can recognize instantly a poor director if such is his arrangement. Perspectivizing then is the first characteristic of the spatial relationship between A and B.

The other important rule is that action involving any sort of displacement (like sitting, standing, moving) should take place while the character involved is *on* the screen, that is: if a shot of A wearing a top hat is followed by a shot of B, lasting ten seconds, then A should still have his hat on the next time we see him, even though, in real time, during the ten seconds B was on the screen, A *had* time to take the hat off. The only compositionally correct way for A to become hatless would require him to begin removing the hat in his first appearance. In such a case he would have to be holding his hat when he is next seen. A different example of arranging a displacement according to this rule can be seen in the analysis of Renior's *Grand Illusion* later in this chapter.

The rationale for this rule is that in separation there is a *simultaneity* of action of the participants, rather than a parallelism. Any action that takes place off screen is out of the viewer's range and irretrievable. In order to properly "match" the sequence the viewer must see everything in stable images without displacements. The illusion of reality in separation is so fragile that it should not be disturbed by unexplained changes. Conversely, when the images are stable, the viewer is able to perform all sorts of mental-visual gymnastics, providing the sequence of shots is properly manipulated. To demonstrate, I shall again use this hypothetical scene: Shot 1: A looking (close-up), Shot 2: B looking (medium shot); Shot 3: grandfather clock (medium close-up) (Figures 4.1 and 4.2). The first two shots hint that the men are looking at *each other,* but the third shot brings the realization that the men are, in fact, looking at *the clock.*

Spatially, the viewer during the first two shots ingeniously places A facing B. In the third shot, however, the clock challenges the viewer to rearrange that positioning and in effect *turn* the two men to face the clock. Geographically, a third, hypothetical positioning has been established through separate, consecutive images.

The screen position of the men is the *same* in both instances. The introduction of the clock makes them "turn," in the mind of the viewer, without their actually making a move.* In this example, there was no expository shot to indicate the position of the clock in relation to the people. Also, in a classical separation, the above shots would have to be repeated at least three times and a resolution wide shot added at the end. Spatial relations in separation are open-ended for mental transformations, regardless of the actual position of actors in the separate images. Instead, those relations depend upon the *sequence* of images. If the close-up of the student in Eisenstein's Odessa Steps scene (chapter 3) had been followed by a shot of the woman in pince nez, rather than by the rolling carriage, the student would have appeared to be facing the woman rather than the baby carriage. The viewer is allowed great flexibility in interpreting consecutive screen images, assuming that the filmmaker avails himself of that potential. Such spatial displacements are possible only in a series of pure separation shots.

Another rule of separation's spatial facet is that the actors in a sequence must by implication have *eye contact* with each other, and not be gazing into space. This is accomplished with a five-degree "cheat," (5° to the right, 5° to the left; or vice versa). For better interacting, the director usually places A by the sides and back of the camera while shooting B, so that B can look at and react to his offscreen partner.

Graphic arrangements are not necessarily limited to the face-on shots (as in our hypothetical examples). Hitchcock used a *profile* medium shot of Cary Grant implying that he was "facing" a *frontal* close-up of Ingrid Bergman in a park-bench scene in *Notorious* (1946). After several shots, the profile of Grant was changed to a frontal shot, then back again and so on. This arrangement proved workable and it may be considered

---

*Curiously enough, after establishing the implied look at the clock, there is no way to make the men look at each other again without a turn visible on the screen.

another variant on the audience's mentally turning Grant to face "properly."

Joseph Losey in *The Servant* (1963) also experimented with picture size, which, by convention, is perspectivized but stable (more or less the same through the A,B,A,B cycle). In the tense confrontation scene between the protagonist and his fiancée, each successive shot of the fiancée is closer. While this confuses the perspective, a parabolic mirror on the wall behind the head of the protagonist continues to show the reflection of his fiancée at a single distance. The analysis later in this chapter of a Renoir scene also gives evidence of slight changes in picture size and "profile–frontal shot" combination. The proven convention, nevertheless, is to use consistent image size and more-or-less frontal shots.

Abraham Room, the pioneer in perfecting the element of separation, in his film *Bed and Sofa* (1927), attempted to "penetrate" the space between the separate images with a ball, thrown by the protagonist in one frame, and caught by his friend in the next. Another often used move is: A passes a cup of tea out of the frame, implying that he is handing it to B; in the next shot, the hand of A is seen entering the frame of B, who takes the cup handed to him. Such "penetrations," a way of physically connecting the two images, can be used to achieve amazing dramatic effects. Kurosawa does it with swords in *Seven Samurai* (1954), Renoir with handshakes in *The Rules of the Game* (1939), Peckinpah with punches and guns in *The Wild Bunch* (1969), to name just a few.

The element of separation is not limited to two participants. With more participants, the combination of shots can vary: for example, two people in shot 1, one person in shot 2, again two people in shot 3, and so on. We would call this a 2 to 1 separation. The variants can be of any denomination—3 to 1, 4 to 2, etc.—but they must be repeated in the A,B,A,B, etc. pattern. Classical separation involves no more than two or three people.

Separation, as I mentioned before, usually starts with an introductory shot or shots which pictures the whole situation in a wider view. At the close of a series of pure separation shots comes a resolution, a required overview shot, which acts to stabilize the separation experience. In its form the resolution should avail itself of the dramatic intensity of the previous separate images, unifying thereby the fluency of the sequence: it should not be a mere throw-in to reassure the viewer of the "real" world in which the separation shots floated. Rather the wider resolution shot should provide a gentle step back from abstraction to reality, the way a G minor passage in music may be skillfully resolved back into C major, the primary key of the piece. Adroitness in handling such resolutions shows the craft of a filmmaker.

Rhythm and Apparent Time

In separation, the sense of time is a complex matter. Individual pictures with their precise lengths create rhythmical pulsations, as in all cuts. But the simultaneity and the strength of the separated picture create a lingering "after-image" which holds over from one image to the next. This phenomenon brings into play another kind of time: *the apparent time*, a term drawn from the nautical vocabulary. In nautical terminology, "apparent wind" refers to the wind created by forward movement of a boat. Through proper sail arrangement, this "extra" wind is used, in addition to the "real" wind from the atmosphere, to propel the craft forward. In separation, time is compounded in the sequence of images by the "aura" of that extra after-image. While watching image A, the viewer is strongly and predictably aware of the presence of image B in recurrent cycles. In short, image A receives a "shadow" of apparent time from the previous shot and, in turn, projects an apparent time on the next image B, and so on. It is like applying the hold pedal to sustain a note on a piano.

The more significant an image is (in form), the stronger the apparent time. For example, in the analysis from *Psycho* (1960) to follow, the policeman, truly a "significant form," carries a longer apparent time than Marion.

Dialogue, overlapping from one shot to the next, introduces another range of rhythmical variants, contrapointed in effect of real time (audio) clashing or meshing with apparent time (image).

The general rule of a minimum three shot phrase is broadened in separation by multiplying it by three. With two participants, for example, separation requires a minimum of three sets of A, B's—a total of six shots. The rationale is that the separate shots are contingent upon each other in *pairs*. In cases when more participants take part in the scene, the rule will require that we see *each* of the individuals at least *three* times. This was demonstrated in the dining room scene in Ingmar Bergman's *Wild Strawberries* (1958) in which each of the eleven members of the family was seen at least three times, in separation.

PSYCHO

Shot 1. 22½ seconds. Car with Marion asleep on the side of the highway.

A. Extra long shot and longest in duration. This peaceful introductory shot (A, B, C) is structured without camera movement.

B. Highway Patrol car passes, halts, backs up past Marion's car (note arrows).

C. Patrol car parks behind Marion. (The threat is imminent, but kept at a distance.)

Shot 2. 6 seconds. Long shot of cop getting out of car and approaching Marion's. He casts an ominous shadow. The cut is almost on the same axis. (Condensation of time: note the rhythm of shots 2, 3, 4.)

Shot 3. 3 seconds. Close-up of cop peering through Marion's window. (The thematic question in the viewer's mind is: Does the policeman know anything about Marion's crime, or is it just a routine check?) This question creates suspense (which the fragmentation enhances). Symmetry with shot 5.

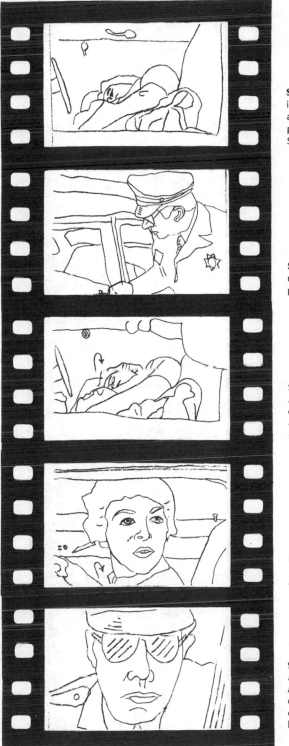

Shot 4. 1½ seconds. Medium close-up of Marion asleep on front seat. This starts a mini-separation (from shots 4 to 8), a prelude to the later pure separation sequence (shots 10 to 27). Symmetry with shot 6.

Shot 5. 1½ seconds. Medium close-up of cop raising his hand to knock on car window. Repeat of shot 3, but the time is cut in half.

Shot 6. 8½ seconds.
A. Medium close-up of Marion awakened by cop's knocking. Her eyes open. Repeat of shot 4. This time the shot continues through Marion's movement.

B. Marion is startled and gets up quickly, moving into close-up. Hitchcock introduces the image A later used in the pure separation.

Shot 7. 1½ seconds. Close-up of cop looking at Marion. Image B is introduced suddenly, not as Marion's in shot 6. This heightens its significance, as does the strength of the graphic and compositional exactitude. The sunglasses heighten the impassivity of the cop.

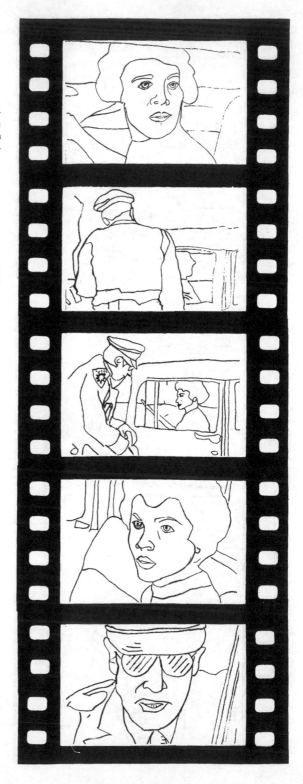

Shot 8. 1¾ seconds. Close-up of startled Marion. Here Marion is an established image A in repitition from shot 6B. The viewer expects a separation to continue. 6B, 7, 8 form a three-beat unit.

Shot 9. 4 seconds.
A. Medium close-up of cop from rear. Marion furtively starts her engine. Cop tells her to slow down and cut it. This objective two-shot interrupts the mini-separation.

B. Medium close-up of Marion as she stops engine. Cop questions her. Introduction to the sequence of pure separation.

Shot 10. 4 seconds. Uninterrupted sequence of pure separation starts with the already familiar close-up. Marion begins to explain. The iconography of both A and B is known to the viewer. The separation will continue until shot 27, in exact a, b, a, b, sequence, lasting approximately 70 seconds.

Shot 11. 1½ seconds. Close-up of cop, listening. Cop's position, features, are virtually unchanging. Perspectivization: cop is a tighter shot than Marion's. Note the displacement of cop from his position in shot 9B.

Shot 12. 6½ seconds. Marion continues to explain. The viewer now begins to anticipate reactions.

Shot 13. 3½ seconds. Close-up of cop.

Shot 14. 3½ seconds. Close-up of Marion. Her expression is more nervous.

Shot 15. 3 seconds. Cop regards Marion somewhat quizzically. The electric current keeps flowing between them. The line connecting them, both in "sensed" eye contact and in the buildup of emotional tension is as tight as can be. Apparent time.

Shot 16. 9½ seconds. Marion continues to insist that nothing is wrong. Tension increases: how much does the policeman know?

Shot 17. 2⅓ seconds. Close-up of cop. Tension of scene increased by the silence when cop is on the screen, except for his own voice when he speaks. Apparent time increases.

Shot 18. 3½ seconds. Close-up of Marion as she turns into profile. Tension relaxed somewhat. Our sympathy is with Marion. The policeman dominates.

Shot 19. 1½ seconds. Close-up of cop. Because of the strength of this image, a deep shadow of apparent time is cast over Marion's image. His shots last 3 to 1½ seconds; hers, absorbing the apparent time, last longer.

Shot 20. 6 seconds. Close-up of Marion. The feeling of greater time value of the B image is apparent; we sense his impression on her.

Shot 21. 1½ seconds. Close-up of cop. How is Marion going to behave under the duress of uncertainty?

Shot 22. 7½ seconds. Marion, who would like to get going, attempts to act cool. Will she panic?

Shot 23. 1½ seconds. Close-up of cop. The viewer works harder while Marion is on the screen; the policeman's image instills only fear.

Shot 24. 2 seconds. Marion prepares to drive off. Will she get away?

Shot 25. 2 seconds. Cop asks to see Marion's driver's license. Peak of tension.

Shot 26. 9 seconds. Marion sees no reason to show her license; she wants to know why it's necessary. She is more nervous than ever. Last shot of A image before the resolution. Apparent time.

Shot 27. 1½ seconds. Cop merely says please very insistently. Last shot of B image before resolution.

Shot 28. 15 seconds. Separations ends with medium close-up of Marion and cop as she digs out her license and hands it to him. An ingenious resolution of the separation by shooting from the other side of the car. Multiangular fragmentation starts. Symmetry with shot 33.

Shot 29. 1½ seconds. Cop goes round to front of car to check license. Symmetry with shot 32. The viewer imagines Marion watching him. Tension is still high, waiting for something to break.

Shot 30. 1½ seconds. Close-up of front license plate.

Shot 31. 2 seconds. Close-up of Marion watching. Symmetry with shot 35.

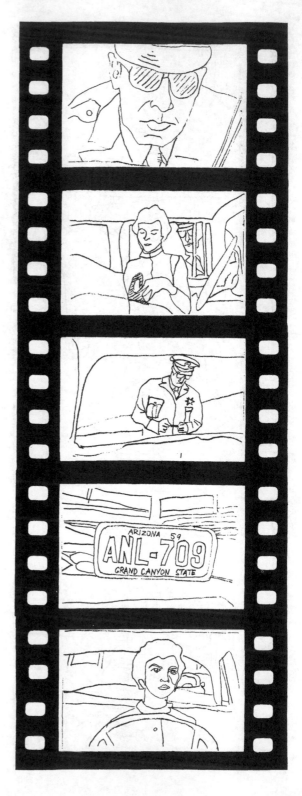

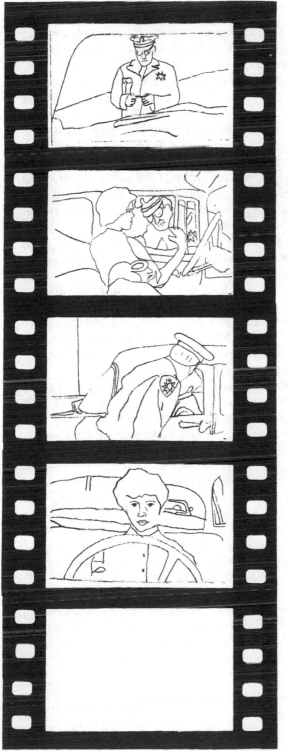

Shot 32. 2 seconds. Cop finishes checking license. Reverse symmetry with shot 29.

Shot 33. 2⅓ seconds. Cop hands Marion her license. Tension eases. Reverse symmetry with shot 28.

Shot 34. 2½ seconds. Sudden reverse as cop finishes returning Marion's license and walks back to his car. A well-camouflaged crossing of the axis. Cop is on right in shot 33 and on the left here.

Shot 35. 10 seconds. Marion, relieved, puts license away, starts up car, and drives off, followed by patrol car. Reverse symmetry with shot 31. Marion takes her time putting away her license, yet cop follows her.

In this magnificently expressive scene, Renoir used the element of separation according to its syntactic rules, understanding its function and its potency. The two aristocrats could not have been in more "intimate" contact with one another. Any alternative (a two-shot on the bench as in shot 2 or an over the shoulder reverse sequence) would have missed the spirituality that Renoir achieved. Structurally, Renoir, after a long shot introduction, locks the separation into symmetry between shots 2 and 21, in composition as well as in camera movement (tracking in and the final pullback out). The small compositional variations during the separation are in conformity with the fluidity of the camera, a touch of cinematic elegance added to the elegance of its participants. The camera's pullback and the fadeout subtly imply a continuation of the thought generated by the scene.

The two analyses give a general picture of how the element of separation is structured and what the rules of its syntax are. Many variants are possible: the following are a few more.

The entrance into separation, unlike the separation itself, is structurally open-ended. It can sometimes be a part of another element. For example, in a group scene structured with multiangularity, one of the participants could leave the group, followed by the camera. A separation could then begin between him in his new position and another person or persons in the group.

In a separation in Chabrol's film Les Cousins, a girl A sits in a chair (medium close shot) while her companion B paces the room throughout their conversation (the camera moving with him to keep him in medium shot). Here we have another variant: camera movements with B: cut to stable images of A; in the resolution: B (pacing) walks over to "A" (stable), the camera following him into a two-shot.

Separation in a traveling car with both participants in the front seat is usually done by showing the driver in profile right and his companion in profile left (a kind of point-of-view shot). An example is George Lucas's American Graffiti (1974). The resolution of the sequence is naturally either a two-shot from the front or side, or a full shot of the car.

A panning shot from one participant to the other can be used only as a resolution to the separation, never in the middle of the sequence. Such a camera movement would break the mystery of the implied space between the separate frames, thus ending the unique quality of separation.

An occasional pair of close shots (seemingly in separation) used as reaction shots or to show short exchanges of looks with or without dialogue are not and should not be mistaken for a form of separation.

Unlike other elements of structure, separation cannot be interrupted. The intangible features of its special reality are an illusion not to be touched. A sequence of pure separation has to be entered, sustained in the predetermined rhythm of the A,B,A,B series, and finally resolved.

The filmmaker must be conscious of all these principles when using separation. Otherwise, the result is a degeneration of the element into those semi-grammatical amorphisms prevalent in the majority of the films.

As a poet is aware of a sonnet's form, a musician of a cantata's, so the filmmaker should be aware of separation as a singular form of expression.

GRAND ILLUSION

Shot 1. 19 seconds. Long shot with deep focus and long perspective. The arched window, the crucifix and the two figures emphasize a dominant horizontal composition. The two officers are strongly lit from above. The wooden-panelled walls blend into the background with soft light and shadows.

The German aristocrat, von Rauffenstein (Erich von Stroheim), on the left and the French count, Boeldieu (Pierre Fresnay) on the right, walk slowly, stopping occasionally, both smoking. A casual conversation is in process . . .

As they approach the camera, Rauffenstein adjusts himself with a slight bend of the knees, a characteristic gesture (an indication of his war injuries). This is the coming separation's overture, a slow, relaxed long shot. Unlike Hitchcock, this is executed via mise-en-scène, by the movement of the participants from the background to the foreground.

This is the last frame of Shot 1. The fluidity of this shot is continued through a cut on movement to . . .

Shot 2. 18½ seconds. 90-degree turn to the side, medium shot. Rauffenstein's figure enters the empty frame, instantly filling half the screen with his silhouette. As he moves on and away from camera, Boeldieu enters. They both walk toward a bench by the window. Structurally, we observe a reverse symmetry of movements. In shot 1, the participants approached camera; in shot 2 they move away toward the background—a complementary and balanced arrangement. To emphasize the fluidity, Renoir starts a brief tracking in of the camera, framing the two participants in the window (the setting for the upcoming separation).

The two officers are comfortably seated, and the camera stops moving. This is the last frame of the introduction.

Shot 3. 9⅓ seconds. Medium shot. Beginning of pure separation. The pace is slow, Rauffenstein looks down, before starting to speak. Note that this shot is in profile, a departure from the classical "face on" shot.

Shot 4. 2 seconds. Medium shot. Boeldieu looks on silently. This second shot of the separation is wider than its companion for proper perspectivization (despite the introduction to the geography of the setting in shot 2). Boeldieu is in ¾ profile (we have so far a full profile "A," ¾ profile "B" combination).

Shot 5. 33 seconds. This is the longest in duration—a monologue by Rauffenstein about the injuries he suffered during the war. He asserts: "But it's the only way left to me to pretend that I'm still serving my country. Burned all over, the reason for my gloves, spine fractured in two places, a silver plate, my kneecap also silver . . ."

Shot 6. 4 seconds. Medium shot Boeldieu listens. B is virtually full face (a change of composition from the profiles of earlier shots). The long (33 seconds) period B was out of frame made this displacement possible.

The miseries of war have brought me these riches

Why did you make me

..an exception

..in receiving me here?

..cause your name is de Boeldieu... eer officer in the French Army.

Shot 7. 5 seconds. Medium shot. Rauffenstein is still talking. Again a compositional change, he, like B, is practically face-on, in a position symmetrical with that of his partner. The slight rotation of camera setups was, in part, prepared for by Renoir's use of the 90 degree turn in shot 2 and the tracking-in of the camera in shot 3.

Shot 8. 10 seconds. Medium close-up. Similar in framing to shot 6, Boeldieu asks a question. His image is stabilized.

Shot 9. 10 seconds. A small change in composition. Rauffenstein is in a tighter shot than before. Both shot 8 and 9 are 10 seconds; the rhythm of the sequence becomes even.

Shot 10. 3 seconds. Tighter shot of Boeldieu, to complement the previous shot of Rauffenstein. Tempo of shots begins to increase.

Shot 11. 4 seconds. Same composition as the two previous shots. Rauffenstein speaks about the two other French officers in the camp (of middle-class origin).

Shot 12. 1½ seconds. Same composition as before. Boeldieu speaks.

Shot 13. 5 seconds. Same composition as before. Rauffenstein speaks.

Shot 14. 4 seconds. Same composition as before. Boeldieu listens. This is the last shot of stable recurrent close-ups (with no change in size), which began in shot 9.

Shot 15. 5½ seconds. Medium shot, slightly low angle. A return to the picture composition of shots 3 to 8. Camera *moves* gently to follow the shift of Rauffenstein towards the potted geranium on the window sill. This change in size, as well as the slight camera pan, reintroduces symmetrically the fluidity of the beginning of the scene.

Shot 16. 2½ seconds. To complement the previous shot (15), Boeldieu is also in a wider frame. The sequence of close-ups is abandoned. Boeldieu listens.

Shot 17. 4 seconds. Same low angle composition as in 15. Rauffenstein is delivering the key line of the scene. Note that Renoir did not choose to emphasize this important line of dialogue with a tight close-up, but strictly adhered to a structure that began with long shots, moved to medium, then to close, and back to medium.

Shot 18. 4 seconds. Boeldieu in same position as in 16. He speaks . . .

Shot 19. 1 second. Low-angle, medium close-up. Rauffenstein asks the question while starting to turn toward the window, a movement he will continue in shot 21.

Shot 20. 8 seconds. Same stable position since shot 16. Boeldieu answers Rauffenstein's question in an elegant but pessimistic tone, then, after a thoughtful pause, he changes the subject, turning the conversation to the geraniums.

Shot 21. 14 seconds. Medium close-up. Rauffenstein continues turning toward window as he speaks. Then he turns toward the implied position of Boeldieu. In the process he comes closer to the camera. The movement ends in his sitting down, on which there is a fast camera pullback into a two shot resolution. The fluidity of this is a culmination of the scene's smooth execution . . . which rounds off in a compositional symmetry with shot 2. This tasteful and effective resolution of the separation happened in the final camera pullback to the 2-shot. The scene ends in fadeout.

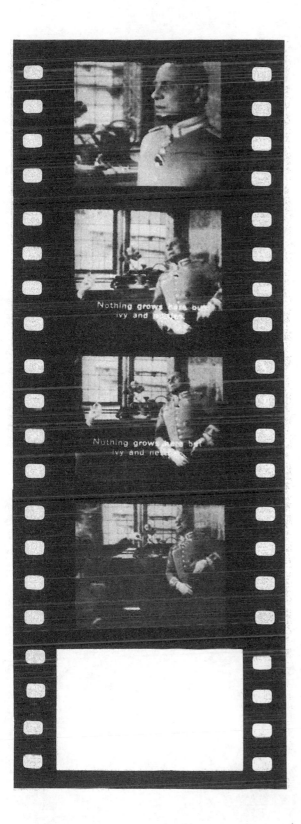

5

Parallel Action

PARALLEL action, another commonly used basic element of cinema structure, generally consists of two narrative lines taking place at a distance from each other. Unlike their geometrical counterparts, however, in the vast majority of cases these cinematic lines do converge after time. Among the usual themes are the search, the pursuit, the rescue, and the chase. These will be classified here as narratively parallel constructions—i.e., those arising from story continuity. There are other constructions more tenuously parallel, in which the two narrative lines occur in close proximity to each other: action in adjacent rooms or upstairs and down, inside and outside a house, in the street or yard, in two cars, and so on. These I shall call adjacent parallel constructions; most often, they are a result of fragmentation. (A wider unfragmented shot could encompass two actions happening near each other, as when two cars in a chase are seen together on the screen.) It should be understood as well that each of the parallel parts are themselves self-contained scenes, with their own variety of cinematic elements, and with their own demands on the arrangement.

I shall discuss first the narratively parallel action, by considering a hypothetical construction. First, a decision must be made as to which action is to be primary and which secondary. For example, in a western the action around the wagon train would be primary while the Indians following at a distance would be secondary. These are somewhat abstract designations, for the question is not the relative importance to the story of one action over the other, but rather how to facilitate proper distribution and emphasis of image elements. By making this division into primary and secondary, the filmmaker engages the two polarities of the cinematic syntax: the ability to *elaborate* and the ability to *condense*. They are powerful complements. Accordingly, and apart from narrative considerations, the primary action is assigned the elaborative function, and the secondary action that of condensation. Whereas the elaborative passages occupy the principal region of the film story, the condensation of the secondary action may, in some instances, create a stronger and more dramatically catalytic passage. Even in cases where the narrative specifically assigns equal thematic impact to the two parallel actions, cinema *must* make the distinction. Without the primary and secondary schemata, the two actions will lose their correlative sense of perspective (as can happen in separation) and will tend to lose their peculiar relationship, thus collapsing the illusion of parallelism.

Another important practice demands that the *point of juncture* between the parallel scenes should be handled in a specific way. The primary action must be a *complete* scene, with a beginning and ending intact, *before* a cut to a secondary action scene is executed. The latter can be more episodic, starting in the middle and ending before a normally integrated scene would. Then, as the story progresses and the dramatic tempo between the two actions increases, a strategically harmonious point has to be found at which the primary action can also become episodic. This usually happens, as a transition, shortly before their convergence. (See the analysis of *Alexander Nevsky*).

The imagery required for the *points of juncture* connecting scenes is specific. In the beginning of parallelism, the last shot of the primary action should be a wider shot (medium or long shot): the secondary should start with a strong, close shot (preferably one that in its repetition on the next round will become a familiar composition) and end in a wider shot filled with energy and *movement*. As the scene recurs, this movement must always be in the same direction. The succeeding primary action will again start with a wider shot—this time with movement in the same direction—where the secondary left off. For example: if in a secondary action the cavalry rides off to the left at the end of the scene, the primary action must begin with the rancher walking to the left, opening a door to the left, executing any movement to the left. The pictorial composition (type of shot and movement) will remain constant, until the convergence of the two actions. Then, in the few scenes preceding convergence, the primary action scenes (now also episodic) will usually end with closer shots rather than the initial, wider ones.

All of the above procedures were observed in an analytical survey of a large group of films in which parallel action was dominant, including masterpieces by Ford, Hawks, Renoir, and Lang; most of them of the western, crime, or police genre.

The main rationale behind the use of a strong close shot at the beginning of each secondary action scene is the need for easy recall. For example, a medium close up of a cavalry captain may be consistently reintroduced to succinctly clue in the viewer that the secondary action is back on the screen. Thus, the medium close shot bridges the gap, however considerable, between the primary and secondary action scenes.

The requirement that primary action begin with a movement in the same direction as that in which the secondary action ended, even though decorative in nature, is so that, again, the two actions are linked. This point of juncture becomes like a subliminal signal for the viewer, even though these movements are actually unrelated. Those subliminal connectors eventually accumulate and carry a considerable amount of narrative and aesthetic value. Connections thus begun are continued as long as the parallel action remains parallel.

Inasmuch as narratively parallel action is usually maintained for long stretches in a film (making a shot-by-shot analysis impractical here), I shall use a chart (table 5.1) to summarize the practices thus outlined. These are classical arrangements; many variations are of course possible.

The time factor in parallel action is quite different from that in separation. Instead of simultaneity, parallel action, in most cases, forms a continuum of consecutive film segments, each scene representing a temporal progression. Furthermore, the film continuity can jump in time during transitions from secondary to primary, and vice versa. This should not be confused with deletions or condensations, useable in any scene, which "economize" on real time by means of cinematic syntax. Skipping time in parallel action is overtly realistic; a scene of a parallel action consumes time so that the next scene has progressed in the meantime. The "in the meantime" concept is at the root of the philosophy of parallelism in cinema, the only exception being a film whose story structure involves flashbacks and flashforwards (like Resnais's film *Je t'aime Je t'aime*—1969). In a sense, these are distant cousins of parallel action.

Skillfully constructed parallelism involves the viewer in a constant awareness of all the actions—those on the screen at the time, and those

Table 5.1   Summary of Action: "Battle on the Ice" Sequence

Primary Action:
full shot   complete scene   *full shot*
————————— different elements —————————
                              Secondary Action: <u>close shot   medium/full shot</u>
                                                  movement ————————————

Primary Action:
full shot   complete scene   medium/full shot
movement →   different elements
                              Secondary Action: <u>familiar   medium shot</u>
                                                  close shot   movement —————————

PRIMARY AND SECONDARY ACTION REPEATS SEVERAL TIMES AS ABOVE

Primary Action episode:
full/medium shot   medium shot
movement →   *Secondary Action:* <u>familiar   medium shot</u>
                                        close shot   movement———

Primary Action: episode
full/medium shot   medium shot
movement →   *Secondary Action:* <u>familiar   medium shot</u>
                                        close shot   movement———————

Primary Action: episode
medium shot/close shot   medium/close shot
movement →   *Secondary Action:* <u>familiar   medium shot</u>
                                              close shot   movement←———————

CONVERGENCE

expected to recur—in a cycle of wishing, hoping or, under different dramatic circumstances, fearing and wanting to delay or forget. Consequently, the rhythm of the succession should not be even. The filmmaker can play on the viewer's tensions by maneuvering the length and the distribution of the parallel scene to make it concur with or differ from the viewer's expectations. If a wide time span exists between two secondary passages, the filmmaker must reemphasize the *recall* value of the imagery, not only through a strong close shot, but also by ending the initial secondary action with a series of significant images powerful enough to span the gap. The recurring secondary action should, in turn, start with a set of images similar to the initial passages, in order to make the recall instantaneous (a fine example is *High Noon* by Fred Zinnemann [1952], who keeps returning to shots of the gunmen, who finally arrive). Counting on narrative explanations (dialogue, letters, or telephone calls) to bridge such a span is hardly as effective as a pictorially powerful suggestion.

Not all narratively parallel action is of the chase and rescue genre, and it often does not have that kind of dramatic intensity. In John Ford's *The Searchers* (1956) two stories run consecutively over a span of several years. The points of juncture are decorated with dissolves, but the basic structure is similar to that indicated in table 5.1.

As an exception, in some cases the parallelism is only implied, and the secondary action "sleeps" until it is shown at the convergence. In David Lean's *The Bridge on the River Kwai* (1957), the protagonist, a British Colonel (Alec Guinness), is placed by his Japanese captors into a hot box and left to suffer in the broiling sun. A long stretch of primary action revolves around that box (including scenes with Japanese commanders and British prisoners who empathize with, struggle, and suffer for their commander). We never see Guinness in the box, however, until later in the film, when he is carried out, half dead.

The same kind of implied parallelism takes place in *Psycho*. The mother, living in the haunted house beside the motel, is never clearly shown: she remains a mystery in the film until the end, when her taxidermically stuffed body is "revealed" in bravura Hitchcockian slow disclosure. In both cases, as in general, a final resolution comes with the convergence of parallel action.*

To illustrate a well structured convergence of parallel action, I will use an analysis of the beginning of the battle on ice in *Alexander Nevsky*, (1938). Eisenstein considered this scene (as well as the Odessa Steps) to be one of the most successful sequences in his filmmaking career. By the time this scene begins, the viewer is already familiar with the participants of both parallel actions: The primary action involves the Russian camp under the leadership of Prince Nevsky and his principal lieutenants, Vasilly, Gavrilo, and Ignat; the secondary action involves the German camp with Ritter Dietlieb, Ritter Hubertus, Von Balk, and the Bishop. The structure of this parallelism was woven on the classical pattern. In the main thrust of the story, the Russians have more time devoted to them than do the German Knights, who are presented in more episodic,

---

*The sole exception of which I am aware is Resnais's *Stavisky* (1974): a secondary action of Leon Trotsky, although parallel, has no narrative connection with the rest of the film, and no resolution.

condensed sequences, with the familiar strong images of tent, monk, and armor at the start of their scenes and with pronounced movement preceding transitions to fuller shots of the Russians. This scene represents the tail end of the parallelism, the point where the two camps are about to lock in battle—a literal convergence of primary and secondary action. It contains 60 shots lasting 6 minutes and 20 seconds (229 feet in 16 mm film). (See analysis pp. 92–104.)

In the summary (Table 5.2) we can see Eisenstein's "brickwork": the distribution of shots within scenes and the formation of consecutive segments of primary and secondary action before convergence. At the beginning of our example, both actions are already episodic; it is apparent that the two camps will soon converge in battle.

Eisenstein orders his shots into three-beat units, many of them on the same camera axis with small compositional variations. Throughout, camera positions are stationary, with one exception—a spectacular crane shot (47) just before the fray. At first, the primary action has more shots; at the end of the series the secondary dominates. Just before convergence, the primary regains prominence. The actual contact between the two camps happens in three stages. The first is in two predictive shots (21, 22) in which we see the Russians and Germans in the same frame (reminiscent of the predictive "mini-separation" in the *Psycho* analysis). Then, after a segment of parallelism (from 23 to 47), the real convergence begins in seven shots (48 to 54); though some distance remains between the troops, it is rapidly shortening. The final stage (55 to 60) is in six shots of the troops locked in battle. Eisenstein delayed the convergence of the two forces for as long as believable, maintaining the parallelism until the last six shots.

In his master plan Eisenstein constructed the convergence of the actions. First he planned the climax, and then the shots leading up to it.* A careful examination of details shows the logic of this method. By knowing exactly the compositional ingredients of his climax, Eisenstein could deliberately order the delicate "tonalities" of the shots leading up to it.

In adjacent parallel action, the two actions take place in immediate proximity to each other over a short time span. Only a few scenes occur before convergence. The most important aspect of such parallelism is that it allows cinema to escape from strict linear continuity. This construction is frequently used and can be seen in many films. In Chaplin's

---

*Personal communication, Alma Ata, USSR, 1947.

Table 5.2 Summary of the Structure

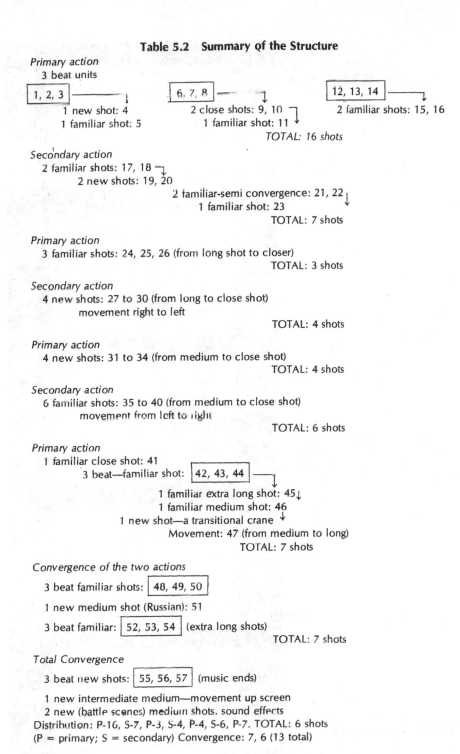

Primary action
  3 beat units

| 1, 2, 3 ─────┐ | 6, 7, 8 ──── ┐ | 12, 13, 14 ────┐ |

  1 new shot: 4   2 close shots: 9, 10 ┐   2 familiar shots: 15, 16
  1 familiar shot: 5   1 familiar shot: 11 ↓

                                              TOTAL: 16 shots

Secondary action
  2 familiar shots: 17, 18 ┐
    2 new shots: 19, 20
                          2 familiar-semi convergence: 21, 22 ┐
                            1 familiar shot: 23   ↓
                                    TOTAL: 7 shots

Primary action
  3 familiar shots: 24, 25, 26 (from long shot to closer)
                                    TOTAL: 3 shots

Secondary action
  4 new shots: 27 to 30 (from long to close shot)
        movement right to left
                                    TOTAL: 4 shots

Primary action
  4 new shots: 31 to 34 (from medium to close shot)
                                    TOTAL: 4 shots

Secondary action
  6 familiar shots: 35 to 40 (from medium to close shot)
        movement from left to right
                                    TOTAL: 6 shots

Primary action
  1 familiar close shot: 41
      3 beat—familiar shot: | 42, 43, 44 | ──┐
                          1 familiar extra long shot: 45 ↓
                          1 familiar medium shot: 46
                1 new shot—a transitional crane ↓
                      Movement: 47 (from medium to long)
                                    TOTAL: 7 shots

Convergence of the two actions
  3 beat familiar shots: | 48, 49, 50 |

  1 new medium shot (Russian): 51

  3 beat familiar: | 52, 53, 54 | (extra long shots)
                                    TOTAL: 7 shots

Total Convergence
  3 beat new shots: | 55, 56, 57 | (music ends)

  1 new intermediate medium—movement up screen
  2 new (battle scenes) medium shots. sound effects
Distribution: P-16, S-7, P-3, S-4, P-4, S-6, P-7. TOTAL: 6 shots
(P = primary; S = secondary) Convergence: 7, 6 (13 total)

ALEXANDER NEVSKY

Shot 1. 9½ seconds. Primary action: Russian side. Fade in, medium long shot. Stormy sky. Three figures on Raven's Rock, a familiar site. Music begins.

Shot 2. 9¾ seconds. Medium long shot. Two figures on Raven's Rock. Slightly high angle.

Shot 3. 9½ seconds. Long shot. Two figures on Raven's Rock. Slightly low angle. Shots 1, 2, 3, are the first of a series of three-shot beats, interrupted by:

Shot 4. 7½ seconds. Extreme long shot. Russian troops on the horizon. A striking horizontal composition after the three verticals.

Shot 5. 7½ seconds. Low-angle long shot. Three figures on the Rock. Repeat of symmetry with shots 1, 2, 3. Change of angle but on the same camera axis.

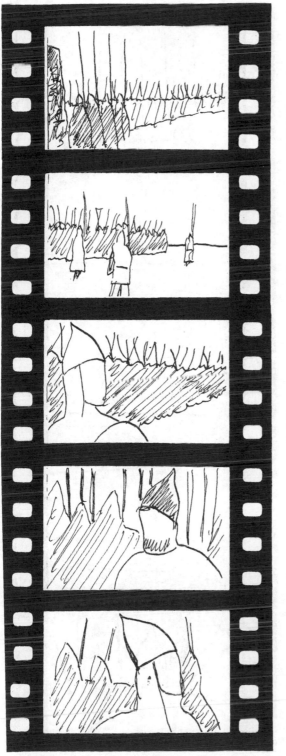

Shot 6. 6 seconds. Medium to long shot, perspectivized. Russian troops at base of Rock, with line extending off to the right. This begins the second three-shot beat.

Shot 7. 6 seconds. Long shot. Continued line of Russian troops. A bit of the horizon is seen on the right.

Shot 8. 6 seconds. Medium to long shot, perspectivized. Vasilly in foreground, Russian troops extending in background to the right.

Shot 9. 5 seconds. Close to medium shot. Ignat facing left with Russian troops in background.

Shot 10. 6 seconds. Close to medium shot. Young Russian soldier facing right, troops in background.

Shot 11. 4½ seconds. Long shot. Russian troops, Rock at right. Reverse symmetry to shot 6.

Shot 12. 4½ seconds. Extreme long shot. The frozen Lake Chudskoye. Beginning of the third three-shot beat.

Shot 13. 7½ seconds. Extra long shot. The bare horizon of the lake.

Shot 14. 8 seconds. Extra long shot. The same horizon of the frozen lake, with a slightly higher camera angle. A prediction of doom.

Shot 15. 5 seconds. Medium shot. Vasilly, Prince Alexander, Gavrilo.

Shot 16. 5 seconds. Medium shot. Russian soldiers stirring slightly. The last shot of the primary action. (Time: 1 minute, 47½ seconds.)

Shot 17. Beginning of secondary action, German side. 10 seconds. Medium shot. German Bishop's tent, a familiar shape and significant form. Priests raise and lower arms, while monks raise and lower crosses.

Shot 18. 4½ seconds. Close shot. German Bishop's tent. He makes several signs of cross, then all raise arms.

Shot 19. 9 seconds. Long shot. German Knights on horseback. All raise gulduns.

Shot 20. 31 seconds. Extreme long shot. Real time. German Knights gallop forward, filling the screen from edge to edge. This shot is the longest in duration in the entire sequence. End of secondary action.

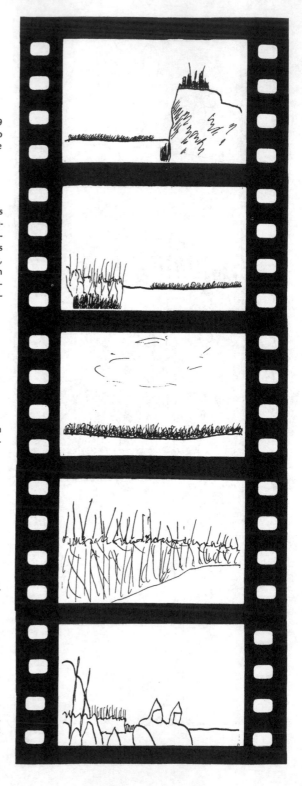

Shot 21. Convergence of the action begins. 9 seconds. Long shot. Russians at the base on top of Rock (right foreground). In the far distance German Knights gallop forward.

Shot 22. 10½ seconds. Long shot. Russian troops on the left, German Knights in the far background galloping on the right. Opposite composition from the previous shot. These two shots are a prelude to the actual convergence. So far, they are the only shots where we can see both Russians and Germans in the same frame. Eisenstein continues the separate actions episodically until shot 48.

Shot 23. 8 seconds. Extreme long shot. German Knights approaching. Symmetry and a seemingly synchronized continuation of shot 20.

Shot 24. Primary action episode. 4½ seconds. Medium to long shot. Russian troops.

Shot 25. 4½ seconds. Medium to long shot. Young Russian and comrade in foreground. Rock and line of Russian troops in left background.

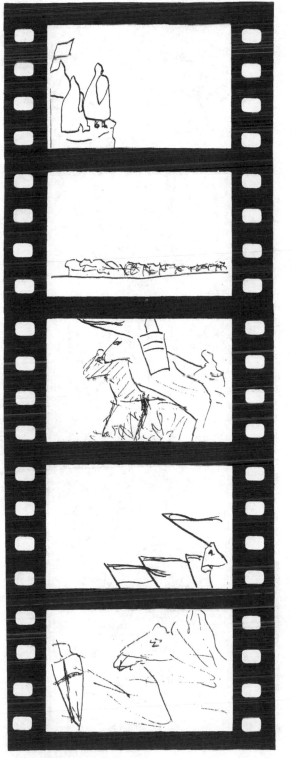

Shot 26. 6¼ seconds. Medium long shot. Prince Alexander and his staff on Rock. Composition farther left than previous shot.

Shot 27. Secondary action episode. 7¼ seconds. Extreme long shot. German Knights advancing right to left.

Shot 28. 5 seconds. Medium shot. German runners, then German Knights advancing right to left.

Shot 29. 4½ seconds. Medium to close shot. **A.** German Knights entering frame right, galloping, as before, to the left.

B. Shot ending in swirling snow on the far left.

Shot 30. 6½ seconds. Medium shot. German Knights galloping in fixed position within frame, as flags travel right to left in the background.

Shot 31. Primary action episode. 3¾ seconds. Close shot. Russian soldiers stirring.

Shot 32. 3⅓ seconds. Medium shot. Russian soldiers.

Shot 33. 3¾ seconds. Medium close to long shot. Young Russian and comrade. Russian troops in the left background. Symmetrical with but closer than shot 25.

Shot 34. 5½ seconds. Close shot. Prince Alexander looking to the left.

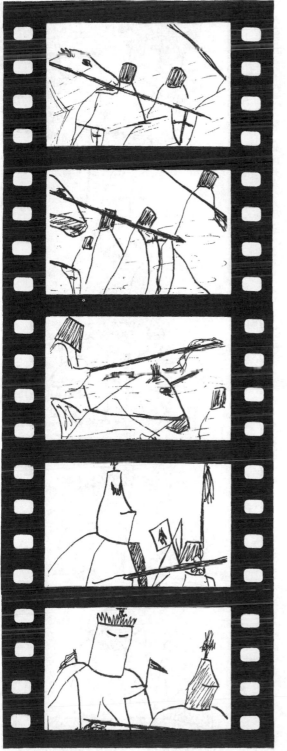

Shot 35. Secondary action episode. 3½ seconds. Medium shot. German Knights enter empty frame, galloping left to right. The radical change in direction of the Germans was made possible by the direction in which Prince Alexander looked in shot 34.

Shot 36. 3½ seconds. Medium close shot. German Knights enter empty frame, as in shot 35, but closer. They gallop left to right as before.

Shot 37. 3½ seconds. Close shot. German Knights again; they enter empty frame. Camera is now perpendicular to the movement of the figures, as opposed to the previous slight diagonal.

Shot 38. 2¾ seconds. Close shot. Ritter Dietlieb on the left, German Knight on the right. Banners moving left to right in the background.

Shot 39. 2¾ seconds. Close shot. Ritter Hubertus on the left. Ritter Dietlieb on the right. Banners in the background moving left to right.

Shot 40. 5½ seconds. Close shot. Von Balk on the left, Ritter Dietlieb on the right and back. Banners moving left to right. From shot 37, each composition turned the principals to face the screen foreground. In this shot Von Balk faces almost front.

Shot 41. Primary action episode. 5 seconds. Close shot. Prince Alexander in a composition complementary to that of Von Balk in shot 40. The Prince raises his arm to drop his face visor.

Shot 42. 10¾ seconds.
A. Medium to long shot. Vasilly, Prince Alexander, Gavrilo. Alexander turns left, walks back, and turns to full front.

B. Alexander speaks: "Time to begin."

C. Vasilly passes behind Alexander to face Gavrilo.

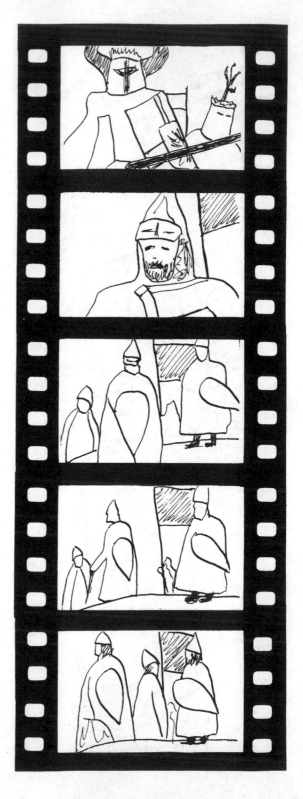

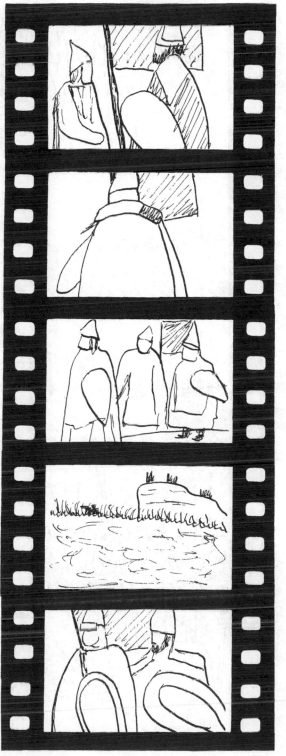

Shot 43. 5¾ seconds. Medium shot.

A. Vasilly and Gavrilo . . .

B. turn to each other and embrace.

Shot 44. 6¼ seconds. Medium to long shot. Same group. Vasilly and Gavrilo disengage from embrace. Vasilly turns and leaves the frame. Small change in camera position from shot **42**.

Shot 45. 9¼ seconds. Extreme long shot. Russian troops at Rock. Horseman moves right to left in front of troops. This long shot is a release from the tension of the previous shot.

Shot 46. 13½ seconds. Medium close shot. Alexander and Gavrilo. Alexander speaks: "Don't hurry. Let the German wedge get in well, and then we'll rush in on them from both sides."

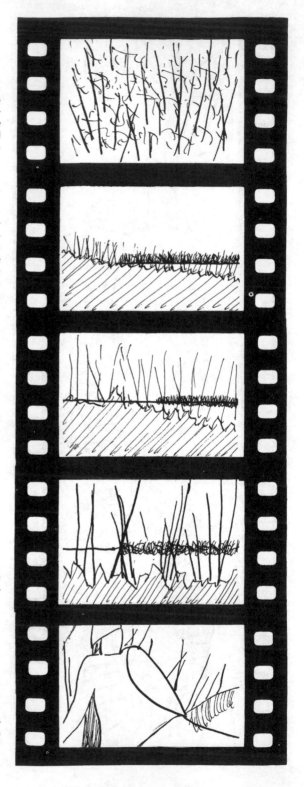

Shot 47. 14 seconds. Medium to extra long shot. Crane shot. The only camera movement in this scene. Shot begins much like 32. The spectacular crane movement lifts camera above the troops to a high-angle long shot. This is the end of the last—and longest (64½ seconds)—episode of the primary action.

Shot 48. Actual convergence begins. 5½ seconds. Extreme long shot. Russian troops in foreground, German Knights, advancing from the background light; since shots 21, 22, we have not seen German and Russian troops in the same frame. Actual contact between the two camps is taking place. This was prepared for structurally by the previous shot.

Shot 49. 5¼ seconds. Long shot. Similar to last shot, but closer and from a lower angle. Russian troops prominent in foreground, German Knights advancing in the background.

Shot 50. 5⅓ seconds. Medium to long shot. Same as 49, closer and higher angle. This is the third shot in three-beat sequence. They are almost identical in length.

Shot 51. 2⅓ seconds. Close medium shot. Vasilly on horseback, draws his sword. Russian troops, in near background, lower their pikes.

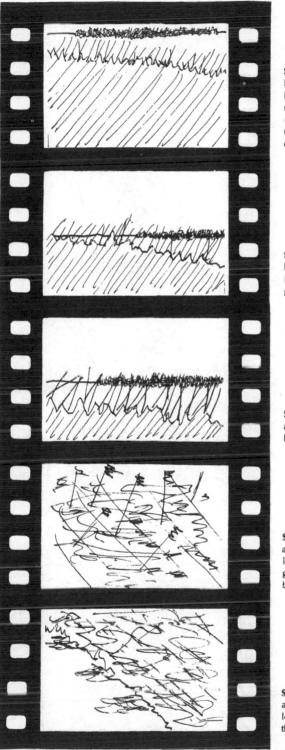

Shot 52. 1¾ seconds. Long shot. Russian troops lower pikes. German Knights advance center background. Similar composition to the one in shots 48–50, but higher angle. This starts yet another three-shot beat. The close shot of Vasilly (51) interrupted two consecutive three-beat sequences of similar composition and rhythm.

Shot 53. 1⅓ seconds. Long shot. Similar to 52, but slightly lower angle. Russian troops, again, lower pikes. Germans advancing in background right.

Shot 54. 1½ seconds. Long shot. Similar to 52 and 53, but from a higher angle. Russian troops lower pikes. Germans closer.

Shot 55. 3½ seconds. Medium to long shot. High angle of German Knights charging from upper left to lower right. Russians in hazy right foreground. This shot starts the last series of three beats.

Shot 56. 3¼ seconds. Medium to long shot. High angle. Similar to 55, but closer and slightly lower. German Knights charging. End of music that began in shot 1.

Shot 57. 6⅓ seconds. High-angle long shot. Russian troops foreground. German Knights attack from upper right and merge with the Russian troops. This is the first physical contact of the element of parallel actions. Note the change of direction in movement. This convergence of the opposing troops is interrupted by the next shot. Sound of horses' hoofs followed by roar of soldiers.

Shot 58. 3 seconds. High-angle long medium shot. German Knights galloping from lower to upper screen. A change of direction. An ingenious use of opposite movements. Sound: roar of soldiers.

Shot 59. 5½ seconds. Medium to long shot. Total contact of opposing soldiers. Battle in progress. Russian soldiers in foreground and in background. Germans in the middle. Battle tones: clanks of armor, hoofbeats, cries.

Shot 60. 4⅓ seconds. High medium to long shot. German troops rush left to right, attacking Russian troops in upper right corner.

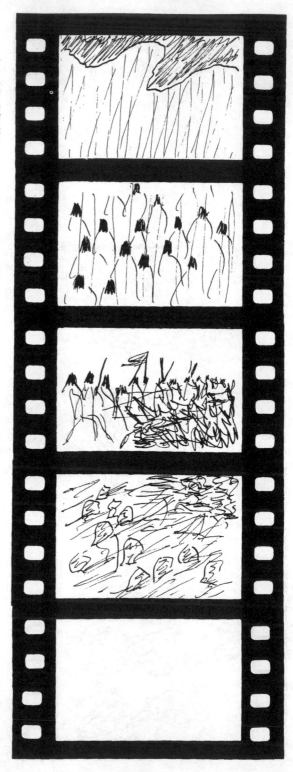

Gold Rush (1925), to name one, the scenes inside and those directly outside the cabin fittingly exemplify adjacent parallel action.

A snowstorm has pushed the fragile cabin to the edge of a cliff, and it starts to tip over the precipice. Inside the cabin we see Chaplin and his friend, Big Jim, sliding down the tipping floor, trying to scramble up to the door, sliding down again, and so on. The next shot of the exterior shows the cabin still on the brink, rocking back and forth, almost falling, then straightening out. The two fellows are controlling the balance with their weight. Several sequences of interior then exterior shots form a classical circumjacently parallel action. If the film had been constructed with interior shots only (the two men sliding and scrambling up) followed by one final exterior shot (revealing the cabin as it tips) we would have had linear continuity, but it would have been far less interesting dramatically. By using parallelism and alternating several times between the interior and exterior shots, Chaplin created a hilarious and touchingly suspenseful sequence. As always in parallel action, this scene ends with a convergence: Chaplin and Big Jim (after the many complications) manage to reach the door and save themselves by stepping out of the cabin just before it falls. The last shot is of the now familiar exterior shot, with the two protagonists in the same frame.

I would like to illuminate further the difference between linearity and adjacent parallelism with a hypothetical example. Imagine a barroom scene in a western with a card game in progress at one of the tables. The protagonist is called away from the game and goes to the back room of the bar, where he meets an adversary. An argument starts which ends in a fight. Eventually, the protagonist rejoins his card game in the barroom. This is a more or less *linear* progression with simple symmetry: barroom, back room, fight, barroom. The same situation could be structured with the elements of parallel action:

(1) the barroom: card game in progress, protagonist called away to the back room.
(2) the back room: start of argument between protagonist and his adversary.
(3) barroom: piano, drinking, card game.
(4) back room: the argument "heats up."
(5) brief barroom scene.
(6) back room: start of fight.
(7) barroom, game table: protagonist returns as if nothing happened, rejoins the card game.

Both versions have identical narrative content. The parallel action, however, "stretches" the story, giving latitude for both elaboration and condensation of the action in the back room. The inserted barroom scenes are incidental, but enhance the action of the backroom action, both in implied time and in intensity. Curiosity is aroused: what is happening in that back room while the action there is "interrupted" by the barroom scenes? The back room argument and the fight gain time during those interruptions.

The same arousal occurred in the *Gold Rush* sequence. While we saw the exterior of the tipping cabin, we imagined the two characters inside, desparately struggling toward the door. Conversely, while watching Big Jim's efforts to climb Chaplin's shoulders on a diagonally pitched floor, we imagined the look of the cabin perched dangerously on the edge of the cliff. We can conclude then that adjacent parallel structures by themselves generate dual attention, which seems to extend the narrative content beyond the given visual information. This permits the filmmaker to accentuate and emphasize, distributing the actions in checkerboard pattern, elaborating on one, condensing the other. The syntactic rules of parallelism govern the characteristic repetitions and eventual convergence. In adjacent parallel action, proximity and brevity bypass the need for the *recall* imagery as in narratively parallel action. Practice dictates that one of the actions, usually the shorter scene, (like the barroom, or the cabin exterior) should be compositionally stable (showing little if any change) and, in most cases, a wider shot. The most fundamental rule is that there should be *several* repetitions (at least three) of the parallel actions in order to plumb the depth of the element. A single "aside," like the linear version of the barroom scene (game table–back room argument–back to the game table), fails to engage the power of dual attention.

A knowledge of the principles and potential of the element of parallelism increases the filmmaker's tools and permits him, when the occasion arises, to turn from strict linearity to the more cinematically expressive parallel action.

6
Familiar Image

THE familiar image as an element of structure has several distinct
forms. It can be distributed throughout a film—thus having the effect
of recalling, like a repeated tune, a picture, likeness, or idea—or it can
be part of a scene, in which case it plays the role of a pivot image.

Any picture which reappears in a film with rhythmic frequency becomes a familiar image, as long as its composition and framing remain
approximately the same. In a self-contained scene, a minimum of three
such appearances are needed. The average number is from five to eight,
the maximum, ten. With more, the vigor of the familiar image lessens
and the device becomes counterproductive. At the end of the structure,
the familiar image is usually integrated into the action of the scene with
a wider shot or through camera movement. This constitutes a resolution.

In a single scene, the familiar image functions as a grammatical conjunction, although, unlike a conjunction in language, it is often repeated
in a given sequence. It acts as a pivotal image around which a scene
or part of a scene is constructed. Always interlocked with other elements of structure, the familiar image nevertheless gives to a scene a
specific architectural format. Like slow disclosure, it constitutes a method
of building cinema sentences.

We know that cinema thrives on repetitions and symmetries. The familiar image structure provides symmetry in the form of a recurrent,
stable picture which "glues" together scattered imagery, especially in
scenes which are fragmented into many shots or involve many participants. When the familiar image is of a leading participant, it acquires

dramatic import as well. Quite often, the image is of a peripheral character, retaining only its conjunctive role, the center around which the dramatic action revolves. Sometimes, such a peripheral image may in the process accrue a meaning of its own, like the ship's doctor's pince nez in *The Battleship Potemkin*.

The origins of this element of structure can be traced to a "bastard" form still persistently used in films: the so-called cutaway shot. When fragmentation into shots became prevalent, a need arose for extra connectors to smooth over "difficult" spots whenever, as a result of mistakes or mismatching, continuity shots did not go well together. Hence cutaways. They were also useful to help with deletions and condensations of action. (During production of a film, cutaway shots were, and still are, accumulated in the editing room—leftover close-ups or specially filmed close-ups of objects on the set, pets, or anything else—just in case they might be needed.) The following scene illustrates the use of a cutaway.

On a suburban street, a man is approaching a house in long shot. The script calls next for a medium full shot of the man on the porch ringing the doorbell. In order to shorten the shot of his walking and at the same time to cover up the awkwardness of an inappropriate camera angle, a close-up of a cat is inserted between the two shots. The result is a manageable sequence: long shot, man walks toward house; cutaway to close-up of a cat at the gate; medium full shot of man already ringing bell. The scene continues on the porch of the house: a woman opens the door and talks to the man. In a proper structure, such a deletion (the long walk to the porch) could have been handled without a cutaway, but under the circumstances it was the best way out.

Let us hypothesize a similar scene in which the cat becomes a structured familiar image: long shot, man walking; close-up of the cat (1) at the gate; medium shot, man ringing bell; repeated close-up of the cat (2); medium close shot, woman in the open door talking to man; same close-up of the cat (3) slowly standing and walking toward woman's feet. The last shot is the "resolution." Use of the cat permits two deletions (walk and door opening) and helps ease changes in picture size and composition, at the same time adding charm without altering or interfering with plot. A single cutaway could have accomplished none of these effects.

The cat is inserted every second shot in the above example, but this is not necessarily the rule. We have merely shown in a brief scene how a cutaway shot may be substituted for an element of structure. Normally, the familiar image is "planted" somewhere in the beginning of a scene, then recurs several times in the middle, with resolution at the end.

Classic examples of the proper use of this element can be found in westerns directed by the masters; here I shall use the first scene in Howard Hawks's *Red River* (1948). A wagon train is heading for Texas. John Wayne and his buddy Walter Brennan decide to separate from the train and continue on to California. The wagon master tries to dissuade them, pointing out the dangers of a lonely journey, but Wayne is adamant. Before departing, he bids farewell to his good friend Colleen Gray, who also begs him not to leave. He kisses her, gives her a bracelet, kisses her again, and starts west, while the main caravan continues south. The scene contains 35 shots and is 4 minutes, 12 seconds long. Shots of Walter Brennan, the driver of Wayne's wagon, are structured as familiar images throughout the scene. Brennan is shown in the driver's seat in medium low angle shot, framed in front of the covered wagon, and the composition remains constant save for movements of body and eyes. The distribution of the familiar image shots is specific: the image is planted in shot 8, recurs in shot 14, 16, 18 (a beat of three, every second shot), and again in shot 28. The resolution, a wider shot, takes place in shot 33, for a total of six repeats. Comment on the detailed functions of this image is included in the following analysis (pp. 110–16).

In this scene the element of the familiar image is structured around Walter Brennan's medium close shot in the seat of the covered wagon. A peripheral character, at least in this scene, he is nevertheless important (starting from shot 8) as a connector of the actions in the vicinity of his wagon. In the absence of a single expository shot showing those actions together in a wider picture, Brennan "connects" the action of the wagon master in front of the wagon with the action of John Wayne and Colleen Gray somewhere behind it. By leaning toward the back (shot 18 and 28), he indicates to the viewer where John Wayne is located. The familiar image of Brennan creates a sense of three-dimensionality by relating to the foreground (wagon master) and background action (Wayne and Gray). He becomes a pivot for the scene. This is the most remarkable feature of the familiar image properly used; it protects the filmmaker from getting into a corner, reminiscent of small prosceniums, with episodic scenes not otherwise tied in with the larger context. Using the familiar image properly, Hawks succeeded in constructing

RED RIVER

Shot 1 (not pictured). Title Card. Fade in. 13½ seconds. The card reads: "In the year 1851, Thomas Dunson, accompanied by a friend, Nadine Groot, left St. Louis and joined a wagon train headed for California. . . ."

Shot 2. 23½ seconds. Long shot. The mountain range in the background. The wagonmaster notices that a wagon has pulled away from the caravan. He rides over to inquire.

Shot 3. 11¾ seconds. Medium long shot. The wagonmaster arrives at the departing wagon. He confronts John Wayne and Walter Brennan. Introduction of the setting of the upcoming familiar image with Brennan in the driver's seat.

Shot 4. Medium shot. The wagonmaster questions Wayne, who tells him of his intention to head alone for California.

Shot 5. 8½ seconds. Medium close shot. Wayne reiterates that he is leaving and that he cannot be stopped.

Shot 6. 3½ seconds. Medium shot. The wagon-master tries to dissuade Wayne, telling him of the dangers of leaving alone. For the next three shots, tempo increases. This shot is repeated in 9, 11, 13, 15, and 17, and represents the stable image of the separation sequence.

Shot 7. 2⅛ seconds. Medium close shot. Wayne in semi-profile, adamant in his decision.

Shot 8. 2¹⁄₆ seconds. Medium close shot. *First familiar image planted.* Brennan in driver's seat, framed by the front of the wagon. He talks to the wagonmaster.

Shot 9. 8 seconds. Medium shot. The wagonmaster and his buddy (on left) warn Wayne and Brennan of the troubles they may encounter.

Shot 10. 14¾ seconds. Medium shot. Wayne continues talking to the wagonmaster. In the background a woman is running toward Wayne. He turns toward her.

Shot 11. 2⅓ seconds. Medium shot. Wagon-master continues his persuasions. This shot helps create a deletion in Wayne's action from 10 to 12.

Shot 12. 3¼ seconds. Medium long shot. Wayne continues the turn he started in shot 10, then runs toward Colleen Gray. The separation sequence ends.

Shot 13. 2¾ seconds. Medium shot. Wagon-master talks to Brennan (out of the frame).

Shot 14. 9¾ seconds. Medium close shot. *Second familiar image.* Same framing as 8. Brennan talks to the wagonmaster while glancing toward the rear, where, presumably, Wayne stands with the woman. This eye movement makes a pictorial connection with the principal action offscreen.

Shot 15. 3 seconds. Medium shot. Wagonmaster same as 13. He still argues with Brennan.

Shot 16. 4⅓ seconds. Medium close shot. *Third familiar image* of Brennan, who continues to talk with the wagonmaster. The function of this shot is again to prolong the offscreen action of Wayne and to connect It with the foreground action with the wagonmaster.

Shot 17. 2 seconds. Medium shot. The wagonmaster starts his horse to screen left, ready to ride off.

Shot 18. 2¹/₆ seconds. Medium close shot. *Fourth familiar image.* Brennan looks to the rear of the wagon, toward offscreen Wayne, making a body movement opposite and complementary to the wagonmaster's (to the left) in 17. Brennan makes a strong connection with the offscreen action.

Shot 19. 4½ seconds. Long shot. Wayne embraces Gray. The sky and mountains frame them in an epic manner. This shot is like a release while the previous familiar image (18) functions like a trigger.

Shot 20. 11⅓ seconds. Medium close shot. Three-quarter view of Wayne in front of Gray as they look at each other. She begs him to take her with him. Wayne is firm in his decision to go alone. The wagontrain moves in the background.

Shot 21. 2¼ seconds. Medium close-up. Three-quarter view of Wayne holding hands. Wayne gently pushes her to leave.

Shot 22. 33⅓ seconds. Close shot. Three-quarter view of Gray. The longest shot in the scene. They kiss. Gray still implores Wayne to change his mind. Finally she realizes he won't give in.

Shot 23. 7½ seconds. Medium close shot. Three-quarter view of Wayne. He remains firm in his decision and confronts her. Wagontrain moves in the background.

Shot 24. 9¾ seconds. Close-up. Three-quarter shot of Gray as she prolongs the farewells. She has sadness in here eyes.

Shot 25. 2½ seconds. Close shot. Three-quarter view of Wayne as he looks down at her. The wagontrain keeps moving. John finally exits to the left. This ends a series of six shots with opposite three-quarter views in two shots.

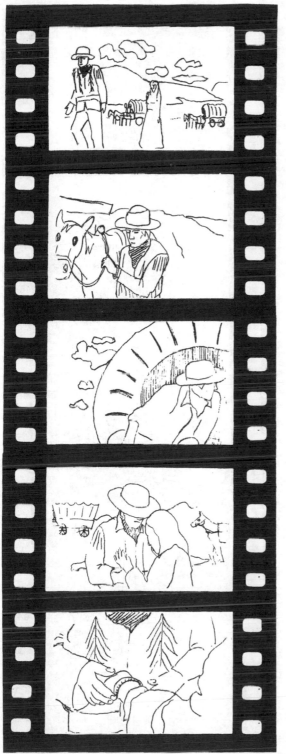

Shot 26. 3¹/₆ seconds. Long shot. Continuation of Wayne's movement, as he walks away leaving Gray in center background.

Shot 27. 7 seconds. Medium shot. Wayne enters from right, reaches for horse's bridle, and moves from screen right to left toward wagon. A bracelet is visible on his hand. He looks at it, then takes it off and exits frame on right.

Shot 28. 3½ seconds. Medium close shot. *Fifth repeat of familiar image.* Brennan in the same composition. He moves his body toward the right again, making a connection with the principal action (while Wayne is off screen), at the same time permitting a deletion in the next shot.

Shot 29. 5¾ seconds. Medium close shot. John enters frame from left. He takes Colleen's hand and begins to put the bracelet on her wrist.

Shot 30. 2²/₃ seconds. Close-up. John slips bracelet on Colleen's wrist. He tells her that the bracelet belonged to his mother.

Shot 31. 17½ seconds. Close shot. At the beginning of the shot, they both look at the bracelet. Then Wayne kisses Gray and begins his exit to the left.

Shot 32. 6 seconds. Long shot. Wayne continues moving to the left and finally exits frame. Gray is left near the center of the frame. Wagontrain moves behind her.

Shot 33. 22½ seconds. Extreme long shot. The mail caravan is moving in one direction, while Wayne and Brennan move toward camera center, Gray still standing in the field. Brennan moves his wagon around her, then to the right leaving her alone. This shot is a resolution of the Brennan familiar image.

Shot 34. 1¾ seconds. Medium long shot. Gray moves sadly. The wagons move behind her.

Shot 35. 22 seconds. Extreme long shot. Brennan's covered wagon in the distance. Wayne waves, then turns his horse around. They leave. Fade out.

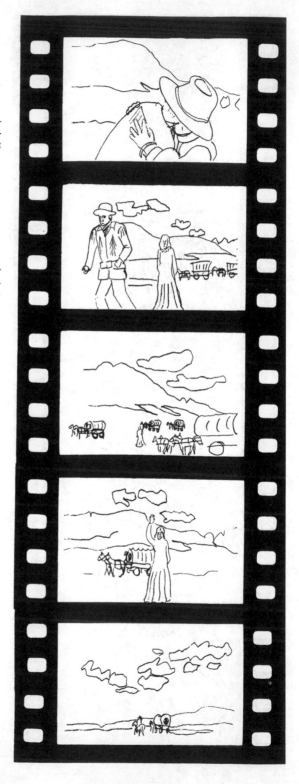

an intimate scene without losing the sense of space of the western landscape. The familiar image creates a "reference" point linking the distant
hills, the wagon, and the intimate action behind it.

The same sense of three-dimensionality and feeling of multi-level space
is achieved in Yasujiro Ozu's *Late Spring* (1948) through the use of a
familiar image of a corridor in the protagonist's house. The corridor
reappears frequently (in the same composition), and the participants in
the drama come and go through it, heading for various rooms. Ozu
starts with the corridor empty; soon, as expected, someone enters it,
passing to the right or left, forward or backward, or from the main doorway off screen. Not only does this shot help us perceive the "imaginary" layout of the house, where most of the action takes place, but it
becomes a reassuring image of a sort as well, a friendly sign suggesting
domesticity, and even though secondary in importance as a setting, it is
a nerve center for all the dramatic pursuits in the rooms around it. As
did the example from *Red River*, this familiar image also functions as a
pivot, a connector, an originator of deletions, and an extender of the
notion of three-dimensionality.

A similar scheme, already a convention in most films, is the use of
onlookers as a familiar image in scenes of fast action—fights, games,
races, confrontations, and so on. The practice of breaking up such a
scene by planting and then repeating several times a picture of one or
several onlookers (in similar compositions) contains the four classic elements of the familiar image structure: (1) It helps connect fragmented
sections of the action, permitting thereby a variety of camera angles
including configurations otherwise realisticly impossible (direct hits of
bullets or punches, spectacular falls, crashes, and the like). (2) It makes
possible deletions in the action "covered" by the familiar image, which
in turn allows for acceleration or deceleration of tempo. (3) It contributes to the believability of screen action by making the viewer see
through the eyes of the "familiar" onlooker in the midst of the action.
The familiar image becomes an additional primer of the audience's
emotional attitudes. The reaction of the on-screen spectator to what he,
but not the audience, sees (the action being "hidden" by the picture of
the familiar image) guides the viewer's response. The onlooker adds to
the excitement by anticipating or filling in on the action. (4) Finally, the
existence of a familiar image structure sanctions fragmentation of a scene
into more intimate shots with a distinct and flexible three-dimensionality
and without an expository shot. The latter usually comes at the end, in
the form of a resolution.

A variant of this structure includes in one scene several familiar images used in succession or sandwiched on top of one another. In such cases one of the familiar images is primary, the others secondary. An excellent example is Eisenstein's Odessa Steps sequence in *The Battleship Potemkin*. The principal familiar image is the woman with the pince nez; the secondary one is the student. By looking over the scene (chapter 3), the reader will easily see that the function of the images is similar to those discussed above.

So far, we have examined the familiar image structure as it appears in a single scene. As stated previously, the other aspect of this element is its use as a recall image spread throughout the entire film or a large part of it. I have discussed recall imagery in connection with parallel action. A recurrent significant image instantly signals a switch to the secondary action. In other instances, the recall image is a dramatically important focal point whose reappearance forms an imminent association with an event or person, bringing back a flood of memories, hopes, or worries, as the case may be: a particular landscape in *Rio Bravo* (Hawks, 1958), a homestead in *The Searchers* (Ford, 1956), a long shot of the factories in Antonioni's *Red Desert* (1964), the view of the French doors—the fatal place of the heroine's suicide in Bresson's *La Femme Douce* (1971), the night scene of the whores' hangout in Fellini's *Nights of Cabiria* (1957), or the sculptured face of George C. Scott as General Patton in *Patton* (Franklin J. Schaffner, 1970). Such images, once properly established in the context of a film, need reappear for only an instant to reestablish their context automatically, even symbolically.

A symmetrically orchestrated distribution of recall imagery is a structure of consequence. The familiarity of an image imbues it with a density of meaning, a compactness uniquely cinematic. A solitary shot of a small gothic window flashed periodically on the screen in *Lancelot du Lac* (Bresson, 1975) means volumes, since the lonely queen lives behind it. All the emotions, struggles, drives, and fanaticisms of the knights, their whole philosophy of life, is tied to this little window. Both structures of the familiar image—the *pivot image* around which a scene is built, or the *recall image* in the larger context—are nonliterary concepts and cannot be precisely "predicted" in a screenplay. They can be conceived only with a knowledge of the cinema syntax within the framework of a master plan.

7

Slow Disclosure

IN essence, one can perceive a succession of filmic images as a continuum of disclosures. Potentially, each new image brings forth something new. As the viewer matches shots into meaningful "sentences," he is also looking for cues in each image on the screen to predict the next one, as if reaching out for the latent image beyond the perpendicular limits of the screen. When the cues are neutral or intentionally misleading, another cinematic dynamic starts operating: the structural element I call slow disclosure. This element functions in various forms.

Like story-generated parallel action, slow disclosure can be conceived of as a particular system of distributing narrative information. Used throughout the length of a film, it involves a prolonged delay in giving away crucial facts in a story, like the secret of Anthony Perkins's mother in *Psycho*. The final resolution occurs in most cases as a tour de force toward the end of the film. Used in this way, slow disclosure is composed of a variety of structural elements. As a story-telling device it is not unique to cinema. It has been practiced superbly in the novel.

As a smaller unit within a scene, slow disclosure starts with a given image, followed slowly by another image of something geographically nearby which sheds a new light on or changes the meaning of the first image. Used thus, it is an element of cinematic structure that divulges screen information according to its own rules. Like the other elements it is unique to cinema in its methods of operation and in its effect on the viewer.

There are two opposing forces at the root of slow disclosure: one, the reality of the initial image; the other, the outer limits of the screen frame containing "hidden" images yet to be seen. When the limits of the frame are expanded, usually through camera movement, these forces clash. Even though the initial image, regardless how limited its scope, has an integrity of its own, there looms a possibility that outside that limited scope lies something unexpected or peculiar which might upset that integrity.

To illustrate, I shall repeat the classic example from Abraham Room's *The Ghost That Never Returns* (see chapter 2). The scene begins with a close-up of the protagonist which is held on the screen for 10 seconds, giving the viewer time to contemplate the man's face and observe his tense features. The man's face is accepted as an interesting fact, a beginning of a flow of information, and it is expected that the story will proceed by the introduction of other shots. At this point, Room's camera starts a slow pullback: we see that the man is sitting on a stool with a grey wall behind him. The camera pulling back through a set of bars to beyond the outside wall then reveals the man to be in prison, seen behind bars in a final long shot. The camera's pullback slowly discloses the man's real condition by expanding the limits of the original frame. Since in the close-up no hint is given of the man's real circumstances, this new information is surprising. One might say that the disclosure is in slight "conflict" with the "integrity" of the initial image.

It is in any case gratifying. Had Room's initial close-up been followed by a cut to a long shot of the prison exterior, the disclosure would have been a fast one, as if jumping out of the limits of the frame into a larger context. The slow disclosure as executed engages the viewer's perception quite differently, slowly expanding the original frame, in real time and under the viewer's scrutiny, by adding new information with each progressing second until the final resolution, the man in prison.

The viewer must rethink the original image and its initial impression as he adjusts to the new situation. Instead of matching shots in progression, as he does in structures involving cuts, the viewer this time is taken on a ride backward, as the reality expands into new meaning. An opposite movement, like a zoom or a camera tracking in from the larger context (long shot of the prison) toward the detail (close-up of a face), would not have required any readjustment of understanding; consequently, such shots are the antithesis of slow disclosure. The only exceptions are cases where the detail when "magnified" reveals important facts unnoticed in the initial long shot—startling features, a disfiguration, and so on.

The principal method in slow disclosure is *camera movement:* a pull-back, a pan, or a combination of the two. It is another instance, so typical of the cinematic structures, of retarding direct expository statements and making the flow of information more complex. This increases the participatory involvement of the viewer, forcing him continuously to reassess previous signals so that they will conform to new ones. Slow disclosure also introduces the element of the unexpected without upsetting the reality of an image, by breaking down the rigidity of the frame and pointing to the existence of life outside its rectangular outlines, cultivating in the viewer a curiosity about that space outside, which remains engaged for some time. Even when cuts later in a scene emphasize the rigidity of the frame, a memory of the slow disclosure makes those outlines suspect; an awareness of the space outside remains. This lingering effect can then be skillfully manipulated either to fulfill or to thwart the viewer's expectations.

There are many variants in structuring slow disclosure through camera movement. In the example from Room, it starts with a close-up, revealing through a camera pullback the prison in long shot. In another instance, slow disclosure might start with a long shot. Picture a large group of people sitting on their luggage at a railroad siding. The camera slowly pans to the right and eventually rests on a close shot of a Nazi soldier holding a submachine gun. As in Room's film, this last shot completely changes the initial situation, even though here it starts with the general and ends with the particular. In Max Ophuls's *La Ronde* (1950), the continuously floating camera executes a series of slow disclosures in a variety of picture sizes and in differing combinations: medium, long, and close shots. The camera follows the protagonist in a dance hall, loses him by floating to some other incident, then quite unexpectedly rediscovers him rushing up a stairway, and so on. In several films by Antonioni, and especially in *The Passenger* (1976), the camera moves slowly and apparently aimlessly from a central position in a given action into neutral space, searching for something crucial yet never finding it. The viewer is put in the position of expecting imminent disclosure, but surrenders eventually to the mood of the wandering camera-eye, realizing that it means pessimism and hopelessness. In this instance, the disclosure is not of a concrete fact which changes the meaning of an initial image, but rather sets a pictorial mood which provokes reassessment of previous imagery. The element of slow disclosure constantly forces reappraisal of prior impressions in a push-pull fashion.

A version of slow disclosure milder than Room's startling revelations is often used as an introduction to scenes. In such cases the goal is less to surprise than simply to unfold a situation in stages, starting with closer shots and then gradually disclosing through camera movement or cuts to wider shots the geography of a setting. This structure touches upon the most important trait of cinema by inverting what would otherwise be easy to comprehend (i.e., the wide photographic proscenium). It starts with particulars seemingly out of context and progressively places them as integral parts of a larger canvas. A close shot of a handshake seen before we know the participants' identities and surroundings has a totally different tonality than does the opposite approach, a long shot of a crowded ballroom followed by a medium shot of two elegantly dressed men and a close-up of their handshake. The reverse order of slow disclosure in such a scene is aesthetically and intellectually gratifying, for it bypasses obviousness for stimulation.

The peculiar satisfaction of sensing, "Aha, I've got it," at a movie is often derived from the element of slow disclosure. Like adjacent parallel action, slow disclosure permits the filmmaker an escape from the straitjacket of linearity. By delicately complicating clarity, it kindles cinematic illusion that is both intelligible and pleasing. In Lang's *M* (1931), scenes of police headquarters and scenes of the underworld both start with extreme close-ups of hands scanning a city map, since both police and thieves are looking for the kidnapper. At first, this device seems disconcerting, for we have trouble deciding whose hands they are. In fact, slow disclosure makes the scenes work magnificently, injecting each with a touch of mystery and comical spice. The scenes from *M* also show that slow disclosure may be used with other elements of structure, here with parallel action. Because of its brevity, slow disclosure is usually connected with other elements, but no matter how brief, its function is both specific and vivid.

Because the principal function of this element is to disclose, it is an open field for cinematic originality; hence, the diversity of approaches. One of them is the rack focus method, which begins with the foreground in sharp focus, usually a close shot, and the background fuzzy and indistinguishable. The camera's slow refocus then brings the background, which contains new information, into focus and leaves the foreground blurry. The same effect can also be accomplished in reverse. The frame size remains constant and the camera stable, while the camera's shift of attention allows a penetration into a part of the frame that was previously opaque. The rack focus method can make mild disclosures, or it can make startling ones; for instance, a sharp close-up of a face with a blurry foreground slowly refocused forward to disclose a barbed wire fence in front of that face may briefly shock us. It may also be used in a more comical vein. Seeing a medium close shot of a pro- tagonist in bed, head resting on a pillow, we expect him to be in bed with his wife (perhaps he has been previously seen in this situation). A refocus toward the blurry background shows to our surprise that he is sleeping beside another woman, now in focus while he is blurry. The rack focus, however, even though effective, borders on trickiness when overused. It must be stylistically integrated with the film's other ele- ments; otherwise, it becomes a cliché.

In another instance, mild slow disclosure "explains" a difficult image which at first elicits misleading associations. For example: an extreme close-up of a forefinger magnified with a macro lens looks on the screen like the sand dunes of the Sahara. A slow camera pullback will show it to be a finger of a hand. A number of such disclosures can be seen in Teshigahara's *Woman in the Dunes* (1954). The deciphering of difficult images via slow disclosure takes place whenever extraneous camera an- gles create purposeful and "decorative" distortions, especially in low angle shots. The disclosure brings the difficult image back to reality in a pleasing manner.

Another variant on the slow disclosure technique achieves its effect without a cut or camera movement. In Chaplin's *The Immigrant* (1917), we at first see Charlie, the tramp, in full shot, back to the camera, lean- ing over the railing of a ship full of seasick immigrants. Charlie's body convulses as if in the spasms of seasickness. After a while, still shaking, he turns toward the camera. He is holding a fishing line with a fish on the hook. We now see the cause of his "convulsions."

Images in mirrors are also the subject of mild slow disclosures. Ingmar Bergman uses them with artistic verve. A frontal close-up of a woman talking to someone off screen is held for a long period. After a while, the woman turns to one side, then around to again face the camera. It then becomes clear that we had been seeing her reflection in a mirror. The gratification of unraveling such a small misunderstanding is char- acteristic of this element of structure. Where else but in cinema do we have to solve a problem of positioning, which for a moment upsets our sense of balance? In the initial close-up, the woman appears to be fac- ing the audience, but when she moves around, we realize that we have in fact been seeing someone with her back to us. In a fraction of a second the viewer must make a mental readjustment of positions in or- der to regain balance. While this may seem a minor matter, readjustments of this sort after contradictory impressions are the life stuff of this cinesthetic element.

The resolution at the end of a slow disclosure sequence is usually for the benefit of the viewer, but in some instances it may also be a revelation for the participants on the screen. The viewer may even be in on the secret before the cast, as in the square dance scene in Ford's *Wagon Master* (1950). A 90-degree panning shot discloses the bad guys riding through the bushes, while the group of celebrating pioneers are unaware of them. The viewer not only sees them coming, but knows of them from a previous scene. Seeing a threat, the viewer is anxious for the pioneers to sense it too. This requires a double disclosure: one for the viewer, the second for the participants. Ford provides it with a low angle long shot in which the dancers finally notice the bad guys. A series of separation shots following elaborates on the disclosure. This analysis begins near the end of the square dance scene (pp. 125–29).

In Milos Forman's *The Loves of a Blonde* (1965), such a double disclosure is bypassed. It is late night and the protagonist, a young musician, is standing with a young woman at the entrance to her apartment building, trying insistently to wangle his way into her bedroom. The woman's attempts to discourage him are hopeless, since the young man forces himself into the doorway every time she tries to enter. In desperation, she promises to let him in through a window so that her parents won't hear them. She enters the building, and the boy waits excitedly for a ground floor window to be opened. A slow disclosure shows the viewer a window opening on the big building's *fifth* floor, with our young woman in it. The boy never looks up, not suspecting that she could have used such a ruse to escape him. He keeps looking into ground floor windows and seeing one open, climbs in, finding himself in the company of a middle-aged couple aroused from sleep. He quickly jumps out and runs down the street; two policemen soon start to chase him. Mid-scene are two repeat shots of the girl watching this comical drama from her upstairs window. Throughout the scene, the viewer is aware of her whereabouts, while the young man is not. It is a scene both charming and funny, and yet one feels a sense of loss, almost of having been cheated: because the protagonist never sees the girl upstairs, the double resolution is missing. It is in the nature of cinema disclosure that assumptions be set aside and ambiguities eventually resolved.

Screen time in slow disclosure has its own peculiarities. When executed through camera movement, it takes place in real time. Yet the timing is arbitrary—exclusively at the filmmaker's discretion. During a

WAGON MASTER

Shot 1. 4 seconds. Medium long shot. Singing is heard on the soundtrack. All the couples continue circling counterclockwise. The vaudevillians' wagon appears in the center background.

Shot 2. 4 seconds. Medium shot. The doctor taps his feet to the music.

Shot 3. 5 seconds. Medium long shot. Disclosure of the doctor in full shot.

Shot 4. 6½ seconds. Medium shot. Jane Darwell drums to the song. The other musicians sit to the left and behind her.

Shot 5. 8 seconds. Long shot. The dancers circle, then stop to bow to their partners. A man in the foreground claps.

Shot 6. 8 seconds. Extreme long high-angle shot. Whooping and song. The dancers begin a grand right and left.

Shot 7. 11 seconds. Long eye-level shot. The camera turns 90° showing the Clegg brothers (the bad guys) entering from the bushes and around the side of the wagon. This is the slow disclosure shot.

Shot 8. 8⅓ seconds. Long shot. Whooping, music fades, silence. At the start of the shot, the dancing continues in a circle. They stop dancing when they see the Clegg brothers. They bow to their partners and look right.

Shot 9. 4¾ seconds. Medium long shot. The bad guys help their leader, Shiloh Clegg, off his horse. They walk slowly forward.

Shot 10. 5⅓ seconds. Medium long shot. Ward Bond, Johnson, Corey, and the Mormon stand in foreground, looking toward the Cleggs. The rest of the dancers clear away.

Shot 11. 3¾ seconds. Medium shot. Soft music. The Clegg brothers in separation from the group of Mormons.

Shot 12. 2½ seconds. Medium close-up. Soft music continues for the rest of the scene. Complete separation. One of the Clegg brothers looks to the left.

Shot 13. 2⅔ seconds. Medium close-up. The second Clegg brother looks at the Mormons in separation.

Shot 14. 3 seconds. Medium close-up, low angle. A third member of the Clegg family looking in separation. Dark sky in the background. The left side of his face is illuminated.

Shot 15. 2.5 seconds. Medium close up. A fourth member of the Clegg family. This is the final shot of the bad guys in close-up.

Shot 16. 2½ seconds. Medium close-up. Presently the Mormons are shown in separation. Ward Bond looks right in the direction of the bad guys.

Shot 17. 2½ seconds. Medium close-up. Ben Johnson looks right.

Shot 18. 2½ seconds. Medium close-up. Harry Carey stands left of center.

Shot 19. 3 seconds. Medium close-up. Another Mormon, who was standing behind Bond in shot 10, looks right. This is the last shot of the series of close-up separation. Four shots of the bad guys and four of the Mormons from shot 12 to shot 19—in the same rhythm.

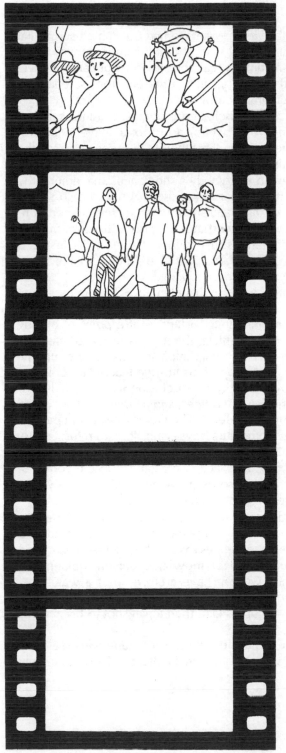

Shot 20. 17 seconds. Medium shot. Shiloh: "Evenin'. Me and the boys seen your fire, and we'd appreciate it if you'd be neighborable. And I heard your mountain music. Said Floyd here, wherever there's singin' and dancin you can be sure there's Christian folk." Same as shot 11. The Clegg brothers in a group shot looking toward the Mormons while Shiloh talks.

Shot 21. 4½ seconds. Medium long shot, low angle. Off screen: "Never did know a bad man that had any music in 'im." Same as shot 10. The Mormons listen while looking at the Cleggs. The symmetry of the confronting groups is completed.

climactic, tense situation, the viewer wants to find out immediately what the resolution will be, but he must wait until the camera movement is completed. Even though the time is real, the slowness of camera travel in slow disclosure imparts a pacing quite different from screen-time elongations made via photographic devices.

Occasionally a dramatic slow disclosure produces a grand finale for an entire film. In the scene from *Psycho,* a turn of a swivel chair discloses the dead body of the "mystery" mother. In this scene, we see the back of an old woman sitting hunched over. Suddenly, the swivel chair is turned around, revealing, to everybody's shock and amazement, the stuffed, dried-up body of the mother in full dress. A naked bulb swinging from the low ceiling casts light and shadow alternately on her monstrous face. Hitchcock superbly orchestrates the preparations for this disclosure as well as the elaborations that follow. The final disclosure is fast; however, both viewer and participants have been waiting for a prolonged period to have the puzzle explained.

Another grand finale with the use of this element is the final scene of Peter Brook's *Lord of the Flies* (1963). The little community of young boys turned savages on an uninhabited island is at a point of bloody hysteria. After killing two in their midst, the gang is ready to massacre Ralph, their deposed leader. The fleeing Ralph suddenly comes upon a pair of shoes, and we see a close-up of his horrified face. He looks up, and the camera starts a slow pan upward, disclosing with painful langor the towering figure of a British naval officer, and a white boat anchored in the distance. The boys burst into tears. The little savages with painted faces, lances, and shields become little boys again, soon to return home, leaving the nightmare behind them. The slowness of the pan as it scans the officer's legs, knees, body, and face is crucial, for in the course of disclosing a God-sent rescuer, it absorbs all the pent-up emotions which at that moment reach a trembling climax.

Both the mild and the dramatic slow disclosure complicate the expository flow of information. Such complication can be regarded as a method in formulating cinema sentences even if the disclosure involved is very mild. For example, instead of showing a person looking at a watch in medium long shot, we can have a close-up of a watch followed by a pan to its owner's face; instead of a full shot of someone writing at a desk, a close shot of his face then a pan shot to his hand as he writes, and so on.

It is important to point out that slow disclosure maneuvers reality in a way that is compatible with the human intellect, which is innately structure oriented and prefers unscrambling a problem to being served the obvious on a platter. That is why this element is preferred by the cinema artists and is an excellent test of their powers of originality. Slow disclosure, of course, should not be overused, but distributed judiciously according to the "score" of the master plan.

8

Cinesthetic Movements:
Moving Camera and Moving Actors

C INESTHETIC movements as a cinematic structure are sequences of
   longer duration incorporating *camera movement, actor movement,*
or, most often, the two in combination, containing characteristic
rhythmical accents. Brief camera movements, occasional walks, or other
displacements of actors in scenes otherwise composed of cuts are not
included in this structure.

The moving camera has been with us since the beginning of film.
Used in a limited way by the early masters (Murnau, Lang, Dreyer, Vertov), the technique has been liberated during the last few decades by
technological advances in camera transport (crab dollies, light cranes),
portable cameras (with gyro stabilizers), multifocal lenses, fast film stocks,
and miniaturized lighting and sound equipment (including radio micro-
phones).* The term "moving camera" encompasses pans in every direction, lifts up and down, crane shots, tracking shots, zooms, and hand-
held floating camera shots, as well as any of these in combination, including process and special effect photography involving movement.

Unlike fragmented sequences of shots from various camera angles,
which convey a sense of compositeness and tridimensionality, the moving camera introduces notions of curvature, circularity, and above all

---

*I believe these improvements are of greater consequence to cinema structure than the
introduction of color, wide screen (CinemaScope), 3-D, or magnetic stereo sound on film.

fluency. Flotation of the camera is a conscious, cinesthetic move not necessarily motivated by a need to depict the reality of any given action. (The only possible exceptions are so-called "point of view" shots, but even these, by the very movement of the camera, perform a function far more complex than merely depicting reality.) The moving camera creates a subjective world of motion. For example, realistic ("objective") movement may be partially arrested by a tracking shot: a walking man will move his legs and swing his arms but does not traverse the screen space—the moving camera keeps him in one spot. The opposite effect is achieved when a seated man is filmed by a camera tracking half-circle around him: he appears to drift in space while in reality motionless in his chair.

Uncommon in daily life, such movements challenge the perceptive faculties of the viewer.* "Reading the text" of a moving camera structure is quite a different process than is the case with fragmentation. There is no need for matching shots, because the floating camera shows all the action as it happens. Instead, the above-mentioned perceptual motor is engaged, resulting in the singular sensation of reconciling illusionary movement with reality. An elegantly executed camera movement emphasizes cinema illusion by taking the viewer on a magical trip which may cover vast territory—over mountains, buildings, or fields—or offer a minuscule introspection—exploring the "landscape" of a physiognomy by slowly circling in close-up around a human face. In either instance the "trip" gives a view normally impossible, but accessible uniquely through cinema.

The above explanation should make clear why this element of structure must operate within a framework of aesthetic originality. Pedestrian camera movement cannot be considered cinesthetic. Repeated zooms into closer shots, often used in the 1970s, are, to say the least, pedestrian and suggest lack of understanding of the function of a camera movement as opposed to a cut. Similarly, someone on the screen may point to the right, with the camera then panning in that direction. Such moves are made merely for the sake of variety. They have no organic or structural rationale.

Most important, the fluidity of a properly rendered camera movement requires that the scene containing it be placed in exactly the right place in the cinematic chain, thus making stringent demands on what pre-

---

*An example from life is the experience of watching from the window of a standing train as a train on the next track moves. It takes a painful moment to realize that it is not one's own train that is moving.

ᴄedes and what follows it. The floating camera by nature evokes a delicate, aerial atmosphere, and the surrounding shots (before and after) must be compatible so as not to break the mood. Usually, a well-chosen significant form precedes and follows such a structure. I shall illustrate this point with two examples, one positive and the other negative.

In one of the most intense scenes of Hitchcock's *Notorious* (1946), we see Alex (Claude Rains), the German master spy, in the wine cellar, as he discovers that his wife (Ingrid Bergman) has betrayed him, apparently giving to a U.S. agent (Cary Grant) the secret uranium ore which had been stored in one of the champagne bottles. In the scene before the moving camera structure, the camera is positioned behind a wine cellar shelf so as to shoot through an array of champagne bottles toward Alex, whom we see in medium close shot, as his hands reach for one, then another bottle, carefully examining their labels. This composition is at once a significant and a difficult image, distorted by the shapes and reflections of the shiny bottles casting dramatic highlights on Alex's face. (The viewer, meanwhile, knows from a previous scene that Ingrid Bergman and Cary Grant have searched the cellar and accidentally broken the fatal bottle of uranium sand.) In the next shot, Alex discovers the remains of the bottle and some scattered sand on the floor—proof of his wife's betrayal.

Then follows the moving camera scene. It starts with a dissolve to a bird's eye view long shot (looking from somewhere near the lofty ceiling down at the large entrance-parlor floor). Alex walks in through a double door, and the camera pans with him as he crosses the large parlor toward the stairway. The camera cranes as he ascends, ending up on the upper landing in an extreme close-up of his face. What starts as an unexpected and startling extra-high-angle long shot terminates in a close-up (somehow symmetrical to the previous close-up in the cellar) by means of an elaborate and graceful camera flotation. We see Alex's tortured face as he tries to decide what to do about his awful discovery; he loves his wife, but must act against her because of her treachery.

The scene following the moving camera sequence starts with another dissolve. In a three-shot staccato (with differing camera angles), Alex is shown in medium shot sitting in a chair. Next follows a separation sequence with Alex's mother, to whom he confesses the truth. The scheme of this arrangement starts with significant imagery in the cellar, followed by camera movement which as a long shot in the beginning performs the function of releasing tension, then builds tension again by craning up to a close-up (an ascent of both camera and emotion), succeeded by a composite view in three shots of the tortured Alex, leading to a separation scene. The moving camera sequence is bracketed by compatible structures; as a result, it is highly successful.

A less successful example of the use of this element can be found in Martin Scorsese's *Taxi Driver* (1976). In the beginning of the film we see a series of elaborate and decorative moving camera shots around the cruising taxi, which culminate in a dramatic circling medium close-up of the face of the protagonist taxi driver (Robert De Niro)—a pleasing and most significant movement. Unfortunately, it is followed by a cut to a master shot of the taxi's full interior, then a cut to a medium close shot of the driver from yet another angle. The switch to these pedestrian shots ruins the impact of the previous camera movements, leaving them hanging, unconnected, and inconsequential. A proper moving camera scene, as I have already indicated, is usually self-contained, and it should be bracketed by compatible fragmented shots of another setting, as is the case in *Notorious*.

The sequence from *Notorious* is to some extent a combination of moving camera and moving actor (or mise-en-scène). A more pronounced unification of these two forms takes place in Renoir's *Grand Illusion* in a longer and more intimate scene of Marechal (Jean Gabin) in his prison cell. A French officer in a German prisoner of war camp, Marechal has made a desperate, but unsuccessful attempt to escape. He has therefore been confined to an isolation cell. Before the scene in question, a short scene shows a group of French prisoners reading an announcement of the capture of another French town by the Germans. A bell tolls and the shot fades out. This is the opening "bracket" before the moving camera scene, which lasts 1 minute and 44 seconds (2,492 frames).

(A few words about the analysis technique [pp. 137–39]: The 2,492 frames of the continuously moving camera are drawn on eight pictures which should be imagined as one unit. Each of the eight pictures is composed of several drawings of individual frames assembled and overlapped to form one image, thus simulating as closely as possible the original span of the movement.)

Immediately following this scene, the outer bracket begins. The guard stands outside the door, listening to the music. After a few seconds, he walks down the hall and passes a young German soldier who asks, "Why did he shout like that?" The old guard answers, "Because the war is lasting too long." The scene fades out with the old guard standing alone at the top of some steps framed by the granite walls of the prison hall-

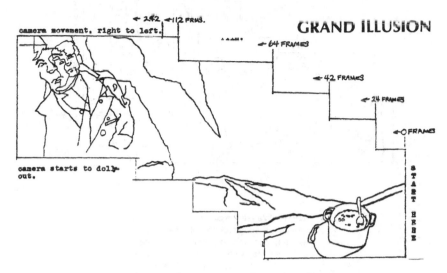

Picture 1. The scene starts with a medium shot of a bean pot. Camera starts panning to the left and up, revealing Marechal in medium close-up sitting alone and dejected on a cot in his isolation cell. At this point (about 10 seconds into the scene) the camera starts pulling back as well.

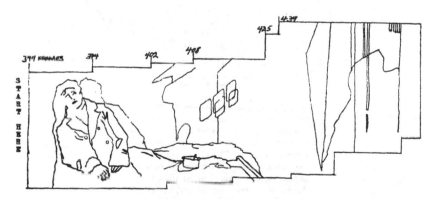

Picture 2. The camera continues pulling back, showing more of the cell, then pans to the right and up toward the cell door. We see the shadow of a figure opening the door and entering.

Picture 3. We see the guard come into the cell. The camera continues to dolly back and immediately commences panning left, while tilting down in step with the guard who walks over to Marechal, and ending in medium shot. We understand that the guard is a benevolent older man when he asks in German, "What's the matter, no appetite today?" He bends over his prisoner and pats him on the shoulder.

Frames 771-796

Picture 4. Marechal answers in French, "I can't stand it here." He stands and runs to the right. The camera follows Marechal, while the guard remains in place. (The two participants switch positions at frames 771–796.) Marechal continues, "I want to see light. It stinks in here." The camera starts its motion to the right, the third change of camera direction and the last major pan in the scene. There is a numerical symmetry in the four camera pans which is balanced by the actors' switch of positions. From here on, camera movements are very slight.

Picture 5. A continuation of the slight pan from picture 4. Marechal speaks: "I want to talk to someone."

Picture 6. Marechal sits down on his bunk, having calmed himself. "I want to hear French spoken again."

Picture 7. The camera dollies in on Marechal. The guard, sitting beside him, tries to console him by offering first candy, which Marechal rejects, then a harmonica, which he accepts. The guard, having demonstrated his compassion for another human being, gets up and begins to leave. He exits frame.

Picture 8. Marechal, alone in his cell, starts to play the harmonica. The camera adjusts, composing him in center frame—the end of the scene.

way. The elegant fluidity of moving camera and moving actors has enhanced the humanity of the relationship between prisoner and guard. Within a cell's small space, Renoir was able to introduce a circularity which symbolically unites the two characters. The term used in the beginning of this chapter—fluency—applies perfectly to this scene.

Some other aspects of the moving camera are discussed in chapter 7, on slow disclosure, in which element the moving camera plays a unique and important role. Subliminal rhythm in this element of structure is achieved by the graphic changes which take place with camera movement, when actors moving from background to foreground change dramatically in size, as in Orson Welles's *Citizen Kane* (1941); when vertical "lines" are created by the camera's passage in a horizontal pan, like the trees in the running sequence in Kurosawa's *Rashomon* (1951); or when there are changes in lighting, pacing, and so on.

There are, of course, innumerable variants in the use of this structure. As stated in chapter 2, the cinematic syntax is a creative force which permits the formation of novel cinema sentences so long as the principal rules are adhered to. In the case of the moving camera and moving actors, these involve subjective movement, circularity, and fluidity, as well as the bracketing of such a scene by complementary significant imagery using other elements of structure. Such a pattern can be observed in works of cinema effectively employing this structure. The films of Alain Resnais are a good example. Experiments using camera movements or moving actors exclusively for a major portion of a film prove unsuccessful. This structure must be interlocked with other elements, even in works where it has a stylistic predominance, like those of the pioneer in this genre, Max Ophuls. One should bear in mind that this structure is not a substitute for cuts, but rather another type of cinema expression; not an alternative to fragmentation, but a complementary mode whose own distinct qualities and functions mesh effectively with other cinematic elements. It should be apparent from this discussion that scenes with shots of longer duration (without cuts) require structuring as complex as those composed of shorter shots.

9

Multi-Angularity

AN autonomous element of cinema structure, multi-angularity is a series of shots of various lengths, depicting a given setting from *divergent camera angles.* It is often a companion to other elements—whether serving as an introduction and/or resolution to separation or a part of parallel action, or interlocked with moving camera, master shot construction, familiar image, and so on. In many instances, though, multi-angularity is a scene's only structural element.

Multi-angularity's most important function is to create an all-enhancing *composite view* of things, through the use of a crisscrossing network of observation points. Because it deals with things in one scene or location at a time, this structure is usually confined to the unity of space, and it should not be confused with continuity shots in diverse locations or with transitional shots, which belong to orchestration (chapter 11). While time progresses in scenes containing multi-angularity, geography remains for the most part unchanging, as the composite view explores a specific area. The only exception to this rule is a variant of this element: the configuration of opposite movements which adheres to the unity of subject. I shall discuss this aspect later in this chapter.

As with the other structural elements, multi-angularity can be considered a cinematic structure only when it contains three or more shots from different camera viewpoints. In the case of a 180 degree reverse angle (crossing the axis), which is normally composed of two shots, the shot or shots before or after the reverse are part of the structure.

To know *when,* for *how long,* and most importantly *where* to move the camera for successive angular views requires much skill and good cinema sense. As mentioned previously, the temptation is to change camera positions for variety's sake, on the assumption that the viewer will tire of one viewpoint and should be exposed to another to revive his attention. Common practice is to use multi-camera setups and shoot from several positions simultaneously, leaving decisions on how to use the various angle shots for the editing room. This method implies a constant rigidity seldom conducive to organic and cumulative compositeness, multi-angularity's principal aim.

A good example of this structure, free from both variety for its own sake and rigid multi-camera setups, is a scene from Ozu's *Late Spring* (1948), already discussed in chapter 7. In the medium long shot which begins the scene, the daughter is squatting, Japanese fashion, with her back to the camera, so that her body completely blocks our view of her father, whom we assume to be sitting across from her at the dinner bench; we see only her grey silhouette in conversation with someone across from her. This shot is sustained long enough to reach the limit of endurance. After 20 seconds, it cuts to a revealing three-quarter view of the two eating their meal, with the father clearly in the frame in a brightly lit medium shot. A tight close-up of his face from yet another angle follows, then a profile medium close shot of the two, smiling happily. The introductory long-duration silhouette shot strengthens the impact of the concluding shot, which expresses, with an explosion of relief, the blissful happiness of a grown-up daughter still sharing a meal with her beloved father before being given away in marriage. Variety for its own sake or a multi-camera setup would never have "discovered" the silhouette angle, for multi-camera positions are usually chosen for repeated use, and here such was obviously not the case.

Multi-angularity, so common in films, is also the structure most often abused, checkmating in most cases the syntactic "rules of performance." In addition to the above-mentioned "angles for variety's sake," which are aimless and frequently pedestrian, there are other cases where multi-angularity is overstructured, as in *The Wild Bunch,* where too many, and too frequent, changes produce the effect of a visual cacophony. In other instances this element used improperly may become a source of disorientation. In many of the outdoor scenes of Elia Kazan's *Viva Zapata* (1952) the viewer must regain his bearing after every change of angle, uncertain if he is still in the same scene with the same characters.

As a final example of misapplication, multi-angularity is sometimes built around given points of view realistically justified by specific circumstances of geography, of action, of characters' looks and attitudes, or by any other narrative requirement. This may be justifiably the case in separation, especially in instances where groups rather than two characters are separated (the latter, incidentally, is often mistaken for classical multi-angularity). The binder in separation is often the eye contact between characters, but even then the particular camera view does not reflect a naturalistically precise point of view of the actors, becoming rather a hint in that direction, the camera angle and framing being subservient to the harmonies of proper image succession.

In well-structured multi-angularity, it would be a fallacy to consider any one point of view as the only rationale for particular camera positions. The very existence of multiple angles within one spatial environment defies the thought that every camera angle is somebody's viewing position, including the audience's. Such an idea is not only absurd from the standpoint of reality: it also goes against the grain of cinematic constructions which, as we have seen, can create a peculiar illusion, free to exercise its "poetic license" of dreamlike associations yet coherent and believable as well. There are many ephemeral points of view in multi-angularity, floating somewhere in suspension ready to be gathered by the viewer, who has no need to know whose points of view they represent.

As a result multi-angularity, common as it is, rarely comes off with flying colors. Hitchcock, Renoir, and Ozu are the unquestionable masters, while Resnais is a very sensitive and searching practitioner. In this structure it is the mixture that counts. The filmmaker must be able to predict the results, like a painter mixing paint or a composer arranging notes into harmony. Furthermore, proper multi-angularity must be planned with a sense of progression, each succeeding shot both illuminating its predecessor and begging for comment from the next one, at the same time cumulatively creating the composite view. In depicting dialogue of narrative importance, changes of angle should not merely visually illustrate a soundtrack; instead, they should follow a construct of their own (as per the master plan) compatible with the style and the spirit of a scene and of the film as a whole. In general, when important plot information is conveyed through dialogue, or if the dialogue is significant in any other way, it should not be interfered with by extreme changes in camera angle, but rather should be left to play itself out in one or two well-chosen compositions. Multi-angularity may serve to introduce such a passage, or to elaborate visually on what is said. Casual or incidental dialogue, on the other hand, can be integrated into a structure of multi-angularity in a partially asynchronous manner: both sound and pictures become elements of screen reality ordered in a specific and complementary way. The following analysis of the opening scene from Resnais's *Muriel* (1962) should illustrate.

Containing 26 shots lasting only 35 seconds in all, this scene has a compactness which nevertheless leaves the impression of a fairly leisurely pace. Most shots last a second or less, exceptions being beginning shots 1 and 4, which are over three seconds each, and the last two shots (25 and 26) of about six seconds each. There is one small camera movement (shot 4) and a longer-duration actors' movement (shots 25 and 26). In addition, the scene contains unexplained hints of a parallel action, seen in shots 2, 6, and 16—close-ups of someone boiling water for tea, which are eventually explained in the subsequent scene. The three shots of parallel action are of no significance here, except in that they add an element of mystery and, by their very presence, break up the pacing and linearity of the scene at hand. Even though the overall structure is multi-angular, setting and characters are introduced through mild slow disclosure, and familiar image is used in five shots (1, 5, 9, 12, and 15) of a close-up of a hand on a door handle. Yet both the slow disclosure and the familiar image are clearly subordinate to the multi-angularity of the scene.

In the course of the scene's 35 seconds, we learn that the middle-aged protagonist, Hélène (Delphine Seyrig), operates a combination antique and interior decorating establishment in her apartment. A woman is shopping for a chest of drawers or a table. In the beginning of the scene, we must assume that the voice we hear is the customer speaking. This becomes certain in the last two shots (21 and 26) when we see and hear her in lip synchronization; otherwise, there is no direct correlation between verbal and visual statements (see pp. 145–51).

During Resnais's 35-second sequence, we see Hélène's establishment and her dealings with a customer. Without being shown all the details, we are offered the essence of the situation: Hélène's detachment and reserve (she doesn't say a word), the objects of her trade, and the hint that the setting is an apartment (tea, stove, etc.). Her customer's behavior illuminates the kind of life Hélène leads. In Sarris's *Interviews with Film Directors* (p. 441), Resnais remarks, "It's up to the camera to find the right way to present the decor, it's not for the decor to conform to the camera. The same thing holds true for the actors." The fragmented multi-angularity creates a compactness without seeming rushed, a composite view which yet seems somehow suspended in time.

MURIEL

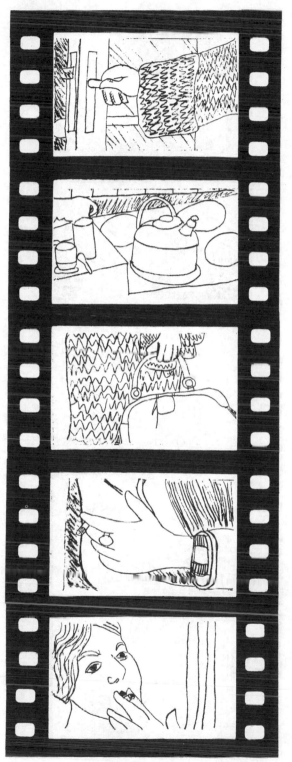

Shot 1. 3⅓ seconds. Close-up. Customer's voice: "What I want . . ." The hand rests on the door handle, thumb tapping lightly against it. This shot will be repeated five times.

Shot 2. 1⅕ seconds. Medium close-up. Still shot of teapot on stove, and utensils. At first the viewer may think this shot is releated to the previous one. Beginning of the three shots of an unexpected parallel action.

Shot 3. ⅔ second. Medium close shot. Another angle and detail of the customer from shot 1.

Shot 4. 3½ seconds. Close-up.
A. Customer's voice: ". . . is a chest of drawers no more than four feet wide." Camera tilts up following Hélène's hand as she lifts a cigarette to her mouth.

B. She inhales. This is the first time we see her face. Camera follows down as Hélène returns her hand, with cigarette, to its position at the start of the shot.

Shot 5. ¾ second. Close-up. Customer's voice: "It has to go between the two windows." Repeat of shot 1, but a little tighter. Her thumb keeps tapping against the door handle.

Shot 6. 1¹/₅ seconds. Close-up. Teapot, water pouring into a cup. It is still not clear what relationship this action has to the previous shots.

Shot 7. ¾ second. Close-up. Chandelier; red curtains in lower left corner.

Shot 8. ¾ second. Close-up. Customer's voice: "If I don't find that . . ." We see the upper part of an elegant chair.

Shot 9. ½ second. Close-up. Customer's voice: ". . . I'll get a teak table." Repeat of shots 1 and 5. This time she does not tap her thumb. By now this shot has become a familiar image and helps connect the different viewpoints of the setting.

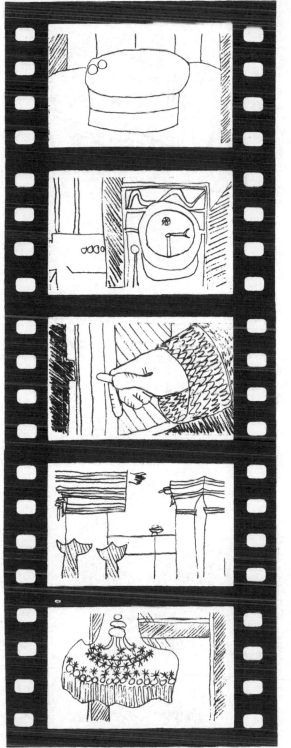

Shot 10. ¾ second. Close-up. A paperweight. Red curtains in the background.

Shot 11. ³/s second. Close-up. Part of a standing clock.

Shot 12. ³/s second. Close-up. Familiar image; fourth repeat.

Shot 13. ³/s second. Medium close-up. Part of a tapestry.

Shot 14. ⅔ second. Close-up. Chandelier in front of doorway.

Shot 15. ²/₅ second. Close-up. Last shot of familiar image of customer's hand.

Shot 16. 1¹/₅ second. Close-up. Last shot of the "mysterious" parallel action.

Shot 17. ³/₅ second. Medium shot. Customer's voice: "Nothing antique." First expository shot with both participants in the frame. Customer's back is to the camera.

Shot 18. ½ second. Medium close-up. Customer in reverse front shot.

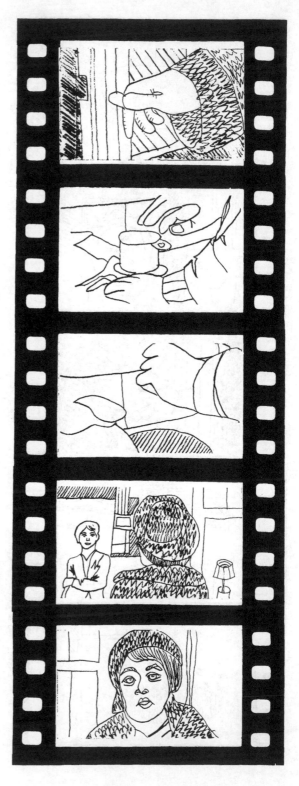

Shot 19. ³/₅ second. Medium close-up. Profile shot of a customer.

Shot 20. ¾ second. Medium close-up. ¾ view of customer's face, clock from shot 11 on the left. This is the third change in the camera's angle on her face.

Shot 21. ½ second. Close-up. Part of her fur coat; red curtain on the left.

Shot 22. ²/₅ second. Close-up. Customer's fur coat from high camera.

Shot 23. ³/₅ second. Medium close-up. Hélène's hands as she lets the measuring tape slide back into a metal box, telegraphing that the visit may be over.

Shot 24. 1¹/₅ seconds. Medium close shot, high angle. Customer's voice: "You have two tastes to satisfy—mine and my husband's." Hélène's legs as she uncrosses them and steps to the right. Persian rug on the left.

Shot 25. 5⁴/₅ seconds. Medium close shot.
A. Customer in lip synch: "I know I can count on you." First on-camera dialogue. She turns and starts walking to the left.

B. Customer turns toward door, ending with her back to the camera. This shot and the next one are of comparatively long duration.

Shot 26. 6²/₅ seconds. Medium long shot.
A. Customer on camera: "The frame must be in good condition." Reverse angle from previous shot; as customer walks and opens the door.

B. She keeps walking, slowly disclosing Hélène on the left.

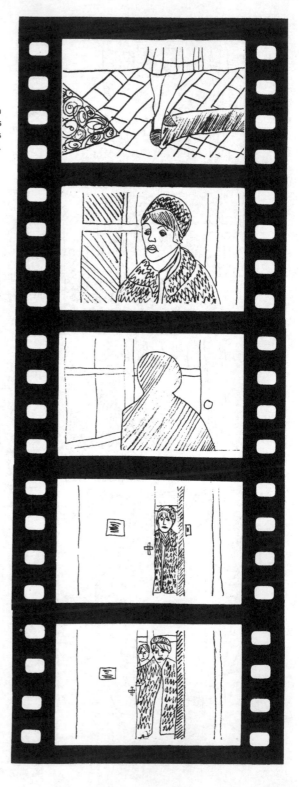

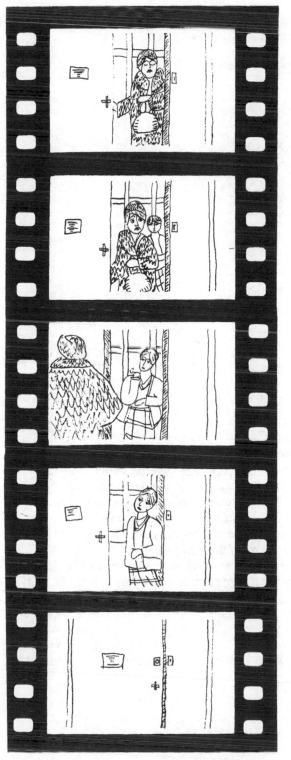

C. Customer steps further forward and for a moment blocks Hélène.

D. Hélène comes into view, this time on the right.

E. Customer walks out of doorway, turns right (counterclockwise) to say good-bye to Hélène. Finally she turns left and walks off the screen.

F. Hélène steps forward, watches the customer's exit . . .

G. . . . then closes the door. Note that in this shot, the longest in duration, Resnais persists in his multi-angularity using movements of actors around the doorway.

The next shot after this scene starts with a close-up of hands with a cup of tea, beginning a new sequence which explains the previous parallel action: Bernard, Hélène's stepson who lives with her in the apartment, is having tea in the kitchen.

Table 9.1. Shot Analysis of *Muriel* Sequence

Shot	Seconds Per Shot	Total Frames
1	3.30	79
2	1.20	29
3	.67	16
4	3.50	89
5	.75	18
6	1.20	30
7	.75	18
8	.75	17
9	.50	12
10	.75	17
11	.60	15
12	.60	14
13	.60	15
14	.67	16
15	.40	10
16	1.20	27
17	.60	15
18	.50	12
19	.60	14
20	.75	17
21	.50	12
22	.40	11
23	.40	11
24	1.20	31
25	5.80	140
26	6.20	155

As with the other elements of structure, multi-angularity needs a resolution, which in this case "wraps up" the diverse viewpoints of the previous shots. Resnais accomplished this in the last two shots of the sequence, which are visibly linear (even though they contain a reverse angle) and of longer duration, thus stabilizing the waves of multi-angularity and bringing the scene to a quieter conclusion. The closing of the door acts as a period, or curtain, to the sequence.

A similar resolution, also two shots of longer duration, can be found at the end of Hitchcock's famous shower scene in *Psycho*. After 67 fragmented shots from divergent angles crowded into the limited space of the bathtub where Marion (Janet Leigh) is murdered while taking a shower, Hitchcock ends the scene with a slow panning shot following the stream of blood from Marion's legs toward the bathtub drain, then zooming in to a tight close-up of the draining water (17 seconds). A dissolve to an extreme close-up of Marion's eye, graphically reminiscent of the bathtub drain, is followed by a slow pullback to reveal Marion's head hanging out of the tub onto the floor (31 seconds).

Another similarity of structure shared by the two scenes is the early introduction of a familiar image: in Resnais's case, the close-up of the customer's hand on the doorknob (repeated five times), and in Hitchcock's the shower head with water pouring out (also repeated five times). In both instances the familiar image serves as a mild introduction to the series of divergent camera angles, connecting them and functioning as an anchor or reference point.

The similarity of structure between Resnais's and Hitchcock's scenes, in the face of diametrically opposite thematic content, indicates once more that the cinematic syntax is, in essence, independent of plot requirements. When a specific structural element is employed, it performs best when it adheres to the rules, yielding a meaning both cinestheticly and narratively valid.

There are, of course, innumerable variants of multi-angularity. My aim here is not to catalogue them—which would be impossible, in any case—but rather to point to mutations which are structurally significant. Two such are *opposite movements* and the *reverse angle* "crossing of the axis" (see glossary).

Opposite movements, already discussed in chapter 2, belong to the structure of multi-angularity because they form a series of shots taken from changing angles. Unity of space is replaced by a oneness of subject. This form usually depicts movement—of vehicles, horses, or people, for example—from divergent viewpoints. In some instances, the subject moves in different directions across the screen, often in opposite directions, yet the sense of progress in one direction remains intact. Take for example a racing train filmed from opposite diagonals and reverse angles. Even though the screen directions change dramatically, the train moving from left to right and then left again, we still understand the train to be proceeding forward to a certain station, not traveling aimlessly back and forth. When well constructed, such a scene actually *reaffirms* a singleness of direction, additional proof that multi-angularity arrives at the composite essence of a situation regardless of reality factors in each separate shot. The whole sequence "plays."

Opposite movements, too, require resolution, a winding down, in a shot or shots of longer duration, of the excitement of opposing movement and changing graphics. Here too a familiar image may be injected at the start of a scene, to be repeated during the action. For instance, in

the case of a woman running down a street in a series of opposite medium and long shots, a recurrent close-up of her face or legs will act as
the familiar image; in the case of a car or train, the windshield or wheels,
and so on.

The strongest variant of this structure is the total reverse angle. Many
filmmakers find it attractive to show certain configurations from both
front and back. Such a change of perspective, as if the viewer is moved
behind the screen, plays havoc with the order of screen directions. When
front and back are cut together, left becomes right and vice-versa. The
audience could become disoriented; hence the rule of "not crossing the
axis," strictly adhered to in Hollywood and elsewhere.*

This golden rule is nonetheless disregarded openly by many directors;
for example, by Ozu in *An Autumn Afternoon* and by Dreyer in *Day of
Wrath*. In each instance, the filmmaker knew that by deciding to cross
the axis he would tamper with reality. In Ozu's film, the protagonist, in
a full shot, is about to sit down on a stool at a bar. As the actor sits,
Ozu reverses (crosses the axis) into a low-angle medium close-up. In
this example, the protagonist, as he sits in shot 1, is facing *left* profile,
but after the reverse shot, 2, he settles down on the stool profile *right*
(in close-up). In Dreyer's film, the protagonist's mother is sitting facing
screen right and talking to her son, the priest. After a brief conversation,
there is a complete reverse into a close-up of her facing in the opposite
direction. In both cases, there is the predictable displacement, but by
skillful use it acquires the strength of an important statement.

This was a new discovery in the use of the element of multi-angularity. The impact of Ozu's scene is strengthened because it is cleaner, a
most obvious orchestration of a reverse. Dramatic emphasis is more
subliminal and at the same time more thought-provoking. The audience
is forced to take notice and think. A strange mystique enters into play
when we see a "flip-flop"—two sides of the protagonist's face, as in a
painting by Picasso—and the simple action of sitting down on a stool
turns into a statement about the character's human condition: it is ele-
vated above the level of mere slice of life. The liberation of the concrete
image from being only a slice-of-life representation is, indeed, a crucial
part of this cinesthetic element of structure. It is as if the camera does
an important part of the acting, revealing the protagonist's humanity not
through picture association or actor's performance but by reversing "the

---

*Even the Army manual for cinematographers has it as the most important of the "do
nots."

order of things." As Chirico said, "a work of art must narrate something that does not appear within its outline."

Total reverse angle (a mirror image without a mirror) is a borderline form, because the principle of not crossing the axis does have some validity. This variant is nevertheless used with skill by the masters, although always with caution and restraint. Even more than the previous variants, this form needs a resolution after the reverse shot to reaffirm the reality of the setting.

To summarize, then, multi-angularity rejects the "proscenium" setting. It dissects an existing but undefined space into a number of triangles, piercing the flat screen from all possible sides. The viewer is deprived of the "rationality" of a central point of view, and in its place is exposed to a triangulation built in an ascending curve toward a composite view of things.

10

The Master Shot Discipline

THE structure I call master shot discipline is an established "Hollywood" method of filmmaking which was perfected and standardized by the 1940s. At that time the advent of sound was changing storytelling methods significantly, putting new emphasis on spoken dialogue and on sound tracks in general. The master shot discipline proved itself a compatible structure, well accommodated to this new development.*

I am not biased against master shot discipline. Its evolution through film history is a legitimate and vigorous construction, a genuine element of the cinematic syntax. Superficially, it may appear to lean toward an overly "naturalistic" presentation of narrative, yet when skillfully designed by such masters as Lubitsch, it becomes an elegant mode of creating screen illusion, singularly cinematic and aesthetically gratifying. Furthermore, the master shot discipline interlocks with other elements of structure. It then performs the function of releasing tension, of creating "the calm before the storm."

This element lies on the opposite end of the syntactic spectrum from slow disclosure; it begins with a master shot, which establishes an objective and stable perspective on a given situation. Often called the establishing shot, it gives a broad view which will then reoccur at least twice in the course of a scene and sometimes more, depending on the length and complexity of the construction.

The master shot may be an extreme long shot of a large area or a

---

* At the same time, it became a congenial system for "assembly line" production of films by the big studios.

medium (long) shot of a smaller situation, usually followed by a series of closer shots which pictorially "magnify" portions of the establishing shot. This effect is executed with a camera dolly or, more often, by a match or "hidden" cut. Take for example a scene which begins with a group shot, one of whose participants is seen lowering himself into a chair. We see the action completed in a medium close shot, so that we hardly notice that the change in picture size—the cut—took place.

This method of joining long shots to closer shots via match cuts is one of the most characteristic features of the master shot discipline. Its aim is to avoid drawing attention to transitions and to achieve a *legato* smoothness in shot succession. The "magnification" of portions of the establishing shot usually progresses in orderly stages of match cuts, from long shot to medium shot to close-up, often on or near the same viewing axis. At this point, depending on the length and complexity of the scene, a variety of configurations may come into play, including other structures likes separation or multi-angularity. Most often, the shot alignment consists of occasional medium shots and so-called *reaction shots in close-up,* all in singles rather than in series—another peculiarity of this discipline.

An analysis of part of a scene from Hawks's *Rio Bravo* (1958) demonstrates this process. The scene starts in the basement kitchen. A gang of outlaws are holding prisoner the innkeeper and his wife while arranging to trap John Wayne: they have tied a thin rope at the bottom of the stairs for Wayne to trip on when going downstairs. It begins with an establishing shot and the camera moves in closer (pp. 159–61).

When two people are shown in conversation, the classic arrangement is the *over-the-shoulder medium two-shot:* a setup three-quarter face toward one of the participants followed by an over-the-shoulder three-quarter view toward the other participant, thus forming an A-B, A-B, etc. semi-reverse two-shot sequence, going back and forth from one speaker to the other. When the over-the-shoulder two-shot system (the opposite of the element of separation) is used for more than four exchanges (four A-B reverses) or is used too often, it becomes the weakest link in the master shot discipline. Proper arrangement calls for an early switch to close-ups, followed by another angle of the two participants. Thus the sequence is freed of the rigidity and monotony of the over-the-shoulder repetitions. Such rigidity, if maintained, is in conflict with the pace of the master shot discipline.

RIO BRAVO

Shot 1. 12.17 seconds. Eye level, medium-to-long shot.
A. This is the master shot. Note that the center is weighted on the outlaw, with Consuella left and forward, innkeeper on the right.

B. Outlaw enters kitchen, dispatches others to the lobby, and then approaches a table to confront Consuella (her gag has been removed).

Shot 2. 2.67 seconds. Medium close-up, eye level. Consuella shakes her head in refusal.

Shot 3. 3.17 seconds. Medium shot, eye level. The master shot, as shot 1, but slightly closer. The familiar image of objects on the table top now acquire narrative importance: the outlaw picks up the bottle in a manner threatening to the innkeeper.

Shot 4. 1.20 seconds. Medium close-up, eye level. Consuella screams. (End of four-shot master shot–reaction shot sequence.)

Shot 5. 3.58 seconds. Medium long shot, above eye level.

A. John Wayne, standing at corner of the hall, hears scream.

B. Wayne looks down. Stairs, rails, and wall produce strong angularity.

C. He rushes downstairs. Note that Wayne does not quite clear the frame.

Shot 6. 7 seconds. Long shot, from below to eye level.
A. Wayne runs along landing . . .

B. Down last flight of stairs and trips on the rope.

C. He flies across the room and crashes to floor. Outlaws converge. Wayne rests left center after fall. Note how the angularity of the stairs, rails, pillars, etc., and the fragmented frame (6A) climaxes in 6B, as Wayne flies through the air. It gives way in 6C to the free-span space of the lobby, where the pattern of the carpet echoes this visual motif.

The following example of properly structured over-the-shoulder reverses is from the last scene of Elia Kazan's *Viva Zapata* (1952). Zapata (Marlon Brando) is arriving at the enemy fort on a friendship mission. First there is an establishing shot followed by a match cut to a typical over-the-shoulder two shot of Brando and the officer. This is repeated five times with reverses. After an excellent structural resolution (shots 7 and 8) Brando, intuitively suspicious, walks toward his horse (pp. 163–65).

The various shots which compose the middle of this structure are followed by the obligatory return to the establishing master shot, which then becomes both a starting point and framework for the action, forming at the end a symmetrical conclusion. This principle of bracketing a scene with its master shots applies both to short and to long sequences. Studio practice is to shoot an entire scene from the master shot position, afterward taking closer shots, reaction close-ups, and details in match with the former, thus permitting a return to the master any time it seems necessary. As a result, scenes of longer duration find the master shot repeated several times in addition to the obligatory bracketing.

This dependence of all the "sub shots" on the "mother" master shot implies a tight ordering, the reason I use the term "discipline." The linearity of the structure is far from helter skelter. Rather, it is built on the solid foundation of a gathering center (the master shot) which radiates an array of decorative asides. The total effect is that of rococo-like architecture.

The master shot discipline is particularly well suited to screen comedy, song and dance musicals, and "light romance," which require a comparatively open frame (more like a proscenium) to play out "the acts" without undue interruption. Gradual, unobtrusive transitions to closer shots leave the impression of a continuing master shot. As for "romance," the majority of Hollywood films feature star actors in romantic roles, and the master shot's gravitation toward close-up helps present screen idols in an intimate way: lingering close shots permit the viewer to indulge in scrutiny.

An integral part of this discipline, the romantic close-up, is a cinematic category in itself. "Through the silk stocking," soft, portrait photography takes its own liberties with reality, because such close-ups do not necessarily match surrounding shots in texture or background. They are special soliloquies, pictorial as well as verbal, during which the dream-like qualities of screen illusion come to the fore. Thought provoking and stimulating, they send the viewer on a path of private dreams not necessarily synchronous with that moment in the story. Then as it recedes via hidden cuts to the medium shot and back to the master, the

VIVA ZAPATA

Shot 1. 385 frames, 16 seconds. Medium-long to medium low-angle shot. Zapata arrives, gets off the horse, and walks through the gate. The officer embraces him. A soldier passes behind them.

Shot 2. 131 frames, 5.5 seconds. Close-up, eye-level, over the shoulder shot.

Shot 3. 101 frames, 4.2 seconds. Close-up, eye-level, over the shoulder reverse shot. Close-up of the officer's face. He stares at Zapata.

Shot 4. 197 frames, 8.2 seconds. Close-up, eye-level reverse shot. Zapata still stares at the officer.

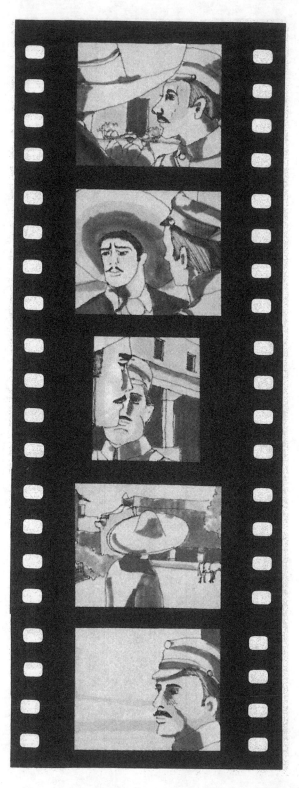

Shot 5. 186 frames, 7.7 seconds. Close-up, eye-level reverse shot. The officer changes eye direction.

Shot 6. 97 frames, 4 seconds. Last over the shoulder shot. Zapata looks around.

Shot 7. 228 frames, 9.5 seconds. Close-up to medium, eye-level shot. Zapata crosses in front of the officer, walks toward the horse, and looks back.

Shot 8. 89 frames, 3.7 seconds. Close-up of the officer's face.

Shot 9. 228 frames, 9.5 seconds. Medium-long, high-angle shot. Zapata walks toward the horse.

romantic close-up, with its strong *after image*, controls dramatically the rest of the scene. Of course, sound track plays a major role in such scenes, neutralizing to some extent the dominance of the pictorial, but never does it affect the integrity and strength of the close-up. Even when it is of a person speaking, the close-up speaks for itself. The sound track, in addition to its dramatic and narrative functions, acts like a bridge, helping to disguise pictorial changes. With the master shot, the sound track dominates a scene's timing (in a more general sense than rhythm), as it descends and ascends to and from its satellite shots.

It is hardly conceivable to think of the master shot discipline as an architectural plan for an entire film. As with the other elements of structure, it is restricted to scenes, and even these can contain other elements as well. There may, of course, be a general stylistic leaning toward the master shot, but even in such films numerous scenes will be composed of other elements. *Ninotchka* (1939) and *Trouble in Paradise* (1932) by Lubitsch have such a leaning, especially in the shorter scenes, while other scenes contain a range of other structural elements. In Hawks's *Rio Bravo* (1959) as well as in other Westerns, a short master shot structure usually precedes an intense or violent scene (built in turn on multi-angularity). Virtually every work of cinema finds it convenient to use a master shot structure for longer scenes with dialogue, as a release, or a pause, or a counterpoint. Still, total dependence on this element may spell theatricality and abdication of the many other rich resources of cinematic expression.

The master shot discipline represents an orderly system as opposed to the chaos of films whose conglomerations of shots aim mainly at communicating raw reality without harmony or elegance. As a source of information about facts alone, the master shot discipline is superfluous; such information is easily communicated in any shot arrangement. But as a construction used deliberately, as an aesthetic and narrative method harmonizing details on a larger canvas, it can result, as it does for Lubitsch, in magnificent cinema.

11

Orchestration

I HAVE defined in general terms the grammatical rules, the characteristics, and the usual functions of each individual element of cinematic structure. We have seen how at times a single element may dominate a scene, while at others several elements mesh. The *basic unit of action* (the scene), while self-contained, is in turn part of a chain of successive units. In cinema, all shots affect one another and whole scenes depend on and influence the scenes around them. This interdependence is not merely progressive: it often operates in a zigzag fashion, a shot or a scene touching upon both a preceding and a succeeding shot or scene, forming a bridge between units of meaning in both a forward and a backward direction. There is, of course, a negative side to this interdependence. An inappropriate resolution may destroy a previous separation or parallel action. An insignificant recall image may fail to recall. A badly structured scene may weaken the impact of what follows. The cinematic chain is a rigorous movement, merciless in its push and pull. It is the function of orchestration to keep this movement under control, tying together a film's various elements and distributing them properly. The aim, ideally, is to achieve an organic continuity which springs from the inner resources of the medium. Orchestration is the guardian of the overall harmonies in a cinematic continuum.

Orchestration's initial responsibility is to present, during a film's first few scenes, the basic iconography of the work, to acquaint the viewer with its "way of speaking," the cinesthetic method which will be employed throughout. An understanding is established between screen and audience, and the audience's perceptive faculties are attuned to the type of "matching" which will be demanded by the film's style and configurations. This is a prelude, mobilizing attention synchronous with the presented structures. Such introductions have been observed in most successful works of cinema.

The next function of orchestration is to control the overall graphic order of things. One aspect of this order is what I call *directional thrust*, when movement on the screen tends to go predominantly in one direction, either left handed or right handed. This should not be confused with the structure of opposite movements (see chapter 9), nor do the two structures conflict. Directional thrust has to do with the distribution of significant movements throughout an entire work so that a "leaning" in one direction results. A film may have one directional thrust until a climax is reached near its middle, and take the other direction from then on; in other cases, like some films of Ophuls, Renoir, or Godard, it may be circular.

The graphic composition of stationary shots can also manifest similar "leanings" when significant forms are consistently anchored on either the right or left side of the frame. A fine point of interest which has been observed in the works of the masters is the opposite leanings of general movement and stationary compositions. The result is internal graphic tension. In the great westerns, for example, general movement and action have a left to right tendency, while the composition of significant stills (in medium shot and close-up) is right handed, as if facing the general movement. In most of von Sternberg's work, still compositions are left handed while movements go from right to left. Lubitsch, on the other hand, avoids creating tension by preferring to combine movement from left to right with compositions which are also left handed. Dreyer too has a left handed tendency for both movement and stable shots, while Eisenstein, Hitchcock, and Bresson prefer playing off opposites. The moving and stationary shots in these examples do not necessarily follow one another immediately: the deliberate graphic uniformities we are discussing occur throughout a film and achieve their effect cumulatively.

Closely related to these graphic leanings is orchestration's next function: the tying together of units of action (scenes). The significant movements or forms which create a directional thrust often play a conjunctive role as well, acting as transitions from one situation to the next. Orchestration determines how this will be done, by creating transitional shots, deploying optical effects (fades, dissolves, etc.), using soundtrack music or sound effects, or by combining these. Music performs a particularly important function in transitions, usually anticipating the end of a scene or telegraphing the next one. Yet in spite of the prevalent use of music, sound effects, and dialogue as primers for the many functions cinema structure can and should perform alone, it does not relieve the pictorial side of its structural requirements.

In the area of transitional shots, orchestration has a task similar to creative editing. As the chain of scenes is formed, new ideas often come from the material itself as it is shaped in shooting, without having been predicted in the master plan. Given the premise (chapter 2) that the cinematic syntax is a creative force able to invent "sentences" never used before, the need to design new transitions is apparent. In practice, this represents a final layer of control at the finishing stages of production. After filmic material is strung together into a rough continuity, adjustments, additions, small changes, and scene connectors are structured in with the aim of sharpening cinesthetic impact.

Naturally, orchestration plays an important part in the formulation of a master plan, especially in arriving at a proper distribution of structural elements. The trigger-release principle, for example, demands that long shots be planted after sequences of intense action. Pauses are created when shots of longer duration are placed after a series of dynamic fragmentation. Screen condensations which normally result in high energy output have to be followed by scenes containing elongations (for release, etc.). In broad, techno-syntactic matters, orchestration assures that certain elements of structure are not overused, that high and low angles alternate, that the distribution of close-ups is well balanced, and so on.

In overall harmonies, orchestration maps out the constant pulsations of symmetries—within scenes, between longer sequences, and throughout a total work. A dexterous use of these symmetries will pay off in an elegant product.

In some ways, orchestration is a superstructure which attends to the ensemble of elements. Many films observe laws of structure fairly well, yet still lack quality. In an ideal situation, orchestration is the effective overseer of quality, because it makes sure that the order of succession and the interlocking of the various elements work to attain maximum cinematic expressiveness.

Conclusion

THE similarities between the inner motors at work in the production and use of cinematic and linguistic structures exist in spite of fundamental differences between language and cinema. Language used with art and sophistication is superior to cinema in its ability to convey abstract concepts, for cinema unaided by language can only provoke thoughts which may approach those concepts. The other side of the coin is language's limited ability to express absolute concreteness. Because word symbols are connected with reality metaphorically, their meaning is always open to interpretation—a subject long pondered by philosophers. Cinema, on the other hand, operates through visual images that reaffirm the very existence of reality. The language of the screen has a limitless vocabulary taken directly from reality and so has no difficulty with concreteness.

The grammatical order of words often aims at defining and clarifying things to bring them close to interesting concreteness and avoid ambiguity. Syntactic order in cinema starts with the concrete as its raw material and builds layers of meaning which may contain interesting ambiguity.*

According to some contemporary linguists, there exists no primitive

---

* A similar "grammatical" order exists in music, but it does not carry a clear communicative message. Rather, it expresses itself magnificently for the sake of expression. In considering the range of similarities shared by music, language, and cinema, the challenging hypothesis comes to mind that music might be the original source of syntactic structures, both linguistic and cinematic.

language as such, all languages being structurally complex and all having to be grammatically rigorous if they are to perform their function of communication. On the screen, however, we can distinguish between two kinds of "language"—one primitive, that of the film without strict organization; and the other complex, that of structured cinema with its nonmetaphoric order of things. Both communicate, but the former is simplistic. It depends on cannibalizing other media and keeps the viewer in a voyeur-like state. Cinema is more compatible with the human intelligence, and it is therefore entitled to be considered a purer "language." A properly orchestrated cinema syntax helps cut the ties that bind film to other media and thus makes it less derivative and more open to cinesthetic innovation.

Much like their verbal counterparts, cinematic sentences reveal information gradually, shot after shot, while the elements of structure, ordering the words of the sentences according to characteristic time-space values, create on the screen a composite view of a world of cinematic illusion.

The screen is the message and therefore the concept of *the screen* is paramount in theoretical considerations of cinema; it is the final "stage" on which occur the "graphic bombardments of the cinematic illusion" and in this context the notion of the camera becomes secondary. The technology of registering the pictorial has developed in recent years to include the electromagnetic as well as the photographic, and it will likely continue to change as new inventions are made. Such technical permutations do not appreciably affect the natural tendency of images on a screen to be ordered. As outlined in chapter 2, the more fragmented an image of a larger reality those images represent, the more they require organization if they are to be expressive. The most important principle in attaining a higher level of expression is that the group of images so organized should generate more meaning than the sum of the information contained in each shot.

Most of our observations about cinematic "syntax" have drawn examples from fictional films. It stands to reason that, with some adjustments, the same ideas apply to other genres as well—to documentary, films of conviction or propaganda, animation, avant garde, and television. Even taking into account differences in production process and type of presentation, there is always a need for order and harmony in pictorial succession, and this is where the elements of structure come into play. Like controlled productions, improvisational shooting of documentary or news footage can also be helped by a knowledge of cinema syntax. A predetermined structural design will guide "improvisations" on film in much the same way as established musical patterns form the foundation for a jazz player's extemporizing at a jam session. In cinema those patterns are the models of structure, open to creative mutations and originality, but patterns nonetheless.

Arising from the inner resources of the film medium, the structural elements have proved themselves the catalysts of cinesthetic expression. All available evidence indicates that the recurring patterns are not merely mirrors aimed at the real world but that they strive to be, like the tree of Leonardo da Vinci, the "sum of its branches," an imagined hypothesis of reality.

Cinema rejects the rationale of literalness, and the degree of literalness in a film is often the key to evaluating the quality of its construction. I have suggested throughout this study that the structures defined here are not simply forms; they also generate content. It is not the obvious, individual image on the screen that counts so much as the mixture of those images, the way they are combined to achieve a kind of synthesis which imbues the "things" shown with a higher import. The viewer is required constantly to negotiate between message and meaning, seen and unseen, hint and fact, engaging both the intelligence and the emotions. Hence the effectiveness of cinesthetic impact depends on its ability to touch upon the essence of things without aiming merely at the things themselves.

Like science, cinema works with a set of facts and has the ability to reduce larger phenomena to primary components. At the same time, cinema, like the other arts, draws its material from mythology. The resulting cinematic experience is the sum of several processes operating together. Visual forms converging with factors of meaning create tensions which must be attended to. Cinema solves the problems of functioning on so many perceptual levels at once through its own specific structures, properly arranged according to the "rules of performance." Those rules are the crux of the "matters strictly cinematic" which I have attempted to illuminate with this study.

In defining and compiling through empirical inquiry the elements of cinematic structure presented here, in prying into "the bricks and mortar" of cinema as it exists today, I have been filled with awe by the genius of the masters and of those film artists who have erected in a relatively short time, from tenuous beginnings, a magnificent edifice of human expression, the importance of which will certainly be recognized in future studies of the humanities.

Glossary

Terms in capitals are cross references defined alphabetically. All terms are explained in reference to their screen effect unless otherwise specified.

ACCELERATED MOTION: A stuffy term for FAST MOTION.

AFTER-IMAGE: An image so graphically strong that the mind's eye retains it even though a new shot has appeared on the screen.

ASPECT RATIO: The shape of the overall picture—so-called because screen shape is identified by the ratio of the screen's width to its height. Screen shapes vary from the normal, nearly square, ratio of 1.33:1 to very long rectangles. (The ratio of most of today's wide screens is 1.85:1.) In the 1950s Hollywood began to compete with various kinds of wide-screen systems, such as Cinemascope, Cinerama, and Vistavision. If a director is preparing a scene which will not look good in a wide-screen format, he may use natural blocking to reframe the image. For example, he may shoot through curtains or doorways that are ostensibly part of the set but appear dark in the foreground.

AVAILABLE LIGHTING: see LIGHTING.

CINEMA VÉRITÉ: An approach to film-making that tries not to interfere with reality. It plays down the technical and formal means of production (script, special lighting, etc.) at the director's disposal and emphasizes the circumstantial reality of the scenes. It often uses natural sound, AVAILABLE LIGHTING, and conspicuous camera work (e.g. ZOOM and HAND-HELD

This Glossary is by Liz Weis and Stefan Sharff with a little help from Reisz and Millar (*Technique of Film Editing*); Gottesman and Geduld (*Guidebook to Film*); Pincus (*Guide to Filmmaking*) and Halliwell (*The Filmgoer's Companion*).

SHOTS), since flexibility is considered more essential than perfection of technique. The term is applied to the documentary work of Jean Rouch, the Maysles, Richard Leacock and others.

CIRCULAR CAMERA MOVEMENT: see SHOT.

CLOSE-UP: see SHOT

CONTINUITY CUTTING: A style of editing marked by its emphasis on maintaining the continuous and seemingly uninterrupted flow of action in a story. However, the continuous time is apparent, not REAL TIME (as within the long TAKES OF CINEMA VÉRITÉ, for example). Contrasted with DYNAMIC CUTTING.

CROSS-CUTTING: Switching back and forth between two or more scenes—for example, a serial episode that alternately shows the heroine nearing the waterfall and the hero galloping to the rescue. Cross-cutting can create PARALLEL ACTION, time, and space. In cases like the above last-minute rescue, excitement and tension are often increased by shortening the shots and accelerating the rhythm of the cross-cutting.

CROSSING THE AXIS: If we draw a line (axis) through the main action of a scene, any camera position on one side of the line will preserve screen direction. If a car is traveling left to right and the camera were to CROSS THE AXIS and shoot from side B, the car would appear to travel right to left. Crossing the axis is a beginner's "no-no" because the results can be ambiguous. However, any number of great directors have proven that they can preserve our sense of a single direction despite the *opposite movements*.

CUT: A TRANSITION made by splicing two pieces of film together. Types of cutting defined in this glossary include: CONTINUITY CUTTING, CROSS-CUTTING, CUTAWAY, CUTTING ON ACTION, DYNAMIC CUTTING, FORM CUT, HIDDEN CUT, JUMP-CUT, SEPARATION.

CUTAWAY: A shot of short duration that supposedly takes place at the same time as the main action, but not directly involved in the main action. For examples of cutaways, see REACTION SHOT and INSERT SHOT. Cutaways are sometimes used less for artistic purposes than to overcome continuity gaps when some footage is bad or missing. If Nixon picked his teeth while speaking, a sympathetic editor would keep the sound but visually cut away to a shot of someone listening that was taken earlier to cover up such routine mishaps.

CUTTING ON ACTION: Cutting from one shot to another view that "matches" it in action and gives the impression of a continuous time span. Example: the actor begins to sit down in a MEDIUM SHOT and finishes in a CLOSE-UP. By having an actor begin a gesture in one shot and carry it through to completion in the next, the director creates a visual bridge which distracts us from noticing the cut.

DECELERATED MOTION: A stuffy term for SLOW MOTION.

DEEP FOCUS: see FOCUS.

DISSOLVE: see TRANSITIONS.

DOLLY SHOT: see SHOT.

DYNAMIC CUTTING: A type of editing which, by the juxtaposition of contrasting shots or sequences, generates ideas in the viewer's mind which were not latent in the shots themselves. Simplified example: shot of man + shot of peacock = idea of egomaniac. Eisenstein thought of MONTAGE as this kind of creative editing.

ESTABLISHING SHOT: see SHOT.

EXPRESSIONISM: A mode of shooting developed in Germany during the 1920s (e.g. *The Cabinet of Dr. Caligari*) which used highly unnaturalistic lighting, sets, makeup, acting, etc., to give a dramatic, larger-than-life effect. Its influence on American films can be seen in Ford's *The Informer* and Welles' *Citizen Kane*.

EXTREME CLOSE-UP: see SHOT.

EYE-LEVEL SHOT: see SHOT

FADE: see TRANSITIONS.

FAMILIAR IMAGE: A graphically strong shot that repeats itself with little change during a film. The repetition has a subliminal effect, creating a visual abstract thought. A familiar image both serves as a stabilizing bridge to the action and accrues meaning as the film progresses. Examples include the "cradle endlessly rocking" in *Intolerance* and the LOW-ANGLE SHOT of Patton against the sky, in *Patton*.

FAST MOTION: Action that appears faster on the screen than it could in reality. Frequently used in the silent film chase. This special effect is shot by running the camera more slowly than usual (e.g., at 12 frames per second instead of the normal 24 for sound films). Since camera and projection speeds were not standardized until the silent era was almost over, we now often see silent films at a much faster speed than we were meant to. Thus we find an unintentional comic effect.

FLAT LIGHTING: see LIGHTING.

FOCUS: An object in focus has a sharp and well-defined image. If it is out of focus it appears blurred. Focus is mainly affected by the lens of the camera, the projector, and your eye.

SP DEEP FOCUS: In deep focus, objects in the immediate foreground and at great distance appear in equally sharp focus at the same time.

SELECTIVE FOCUS: In selective focus, the main object of interest is in focus, the remainder of the objects are out of focus. It is (too) often used when the two lovers gamboling in focus through the fields are photographed through a foreground of out-of-focus flowers.

SOFT FOCUS: In soft focus, often used for romantic effects, all objects appear blurred because none are perfectly in focus. This diffused effect is often used to photograph aging leading ladies. Soft focus can be obtained with filters as well as lenses.

FOLLOW FOCUS: If the camera or the subject moves during the shot, the camera may have to be refocused during the take in order to keep the subject in focus. The procedure is called follow-focus.

SEARCH FOCUS: Also called "rack focus." The switching of focus within a shot from one person or thing to another. For instance, in filming a conversation between two people, the director can place them in the same frame, one in the foreground and one in the background, and alternately keep one in focus, the other out of focus. This is a popular TV effect.

FORM CUT: Framing in a successive shot an object which has a shape or contour similar to an image in the immediately preceding shot. In Griffith's *Intolerance,* for example, the camera cuts from Belshazzar's round shield to the round end of a battering ram pounding the city gates. The circumference and location in the frame of the two circles are identical.

FRAME: see UNITS OF FILM LENGTH.

FREEZE FRAME: The effect in which action appears to come to a dead stop. This is accomplished by printing one frame many times. TV's instant replay sometimes "freezes" a crucial action to let us get a better look at it (but this is done electronically, not with film). Freezes are a popular way to end today's movies, to give an existential feeling rather than a sense of finality. Among the better examples are the zoom-freezes that end *The 400 Blows* and *Wanda.*

GRAPHICS: The formal structured content of the cine-image, as opposed to the haphazard arrangement of the narrative contents.

HAND-HELD SHOT: A shot made with the camera not mounted on a tripod or other stablizing fixture. Since it gains flexibility while it loses stability, it is often used for CINEMA VÉRITÉ.

HIDDEN CUT: An inconspicuous cut, usually used in a fast-action scene, with which the director accelerates the action without significantly shifting the angle or distance as required for a more noticeable cut.

HIGH-ANGLE SHOT: see SHOT.

INSERT SHOT: A CUTAWAY shot inserted for the purpose of giving the audience a closer look at what the character on the screen is seeing or doing; e.g., we see a MEDIUM SHOT of the actor raising his wrist and looking at his watch; then an EXTREME CLOSE-UP shot of the watch face; then a medium shot of the actor finishing looking at the watch and lowering his wrist.

IRIS: see TRANSITIONS.

JUMP-CUT: A cut that jumps forward from one part of an action to another separated from the first by an interval of time. It thus creates geographical dislocation within a unity of space. It usually connects the beginning and ending of an action, leaving out the middle. Godard's *Breathless* created a 60s vogue for jump-cuts.

LIGHTING: The distribution of light and how it models the subjects and affects the graphics is the main aesthetic element of film other than composition.

Light can be *natural* (sunlit) or *artificial* (electric). It can be *flat* (not highly contrasted in brights and darks) or *highlight*. Highlights create dramatic graphic effects. Low-key lighting is recognized by the absence of a strong source of light from a defined direction which creates highlights.

When extra lights are not brought along for shooting, as is often the case with CINEMA VÉRITÉ, AVAILABLE LIGHTING (whatever is normally there) is used.

Most films stocks are not "fast" enough to shoot an ordinary outdoor night scene. So the scene is shot in the daylight and filters are added to darken the scene to look like night. This is called *shooting day for night*. Similarly, there are aesthetic reasons for shooting *night for day*, *exterior for interior*, and *interior for exterior*.

LOCATION: Any place, other than the studio or studio lot, where a film is shot.

LONG SHOT: see SHOT.

LOW-ANGLE SHOT: see SHOT.

LOW-KEY LIGHTING: see LIGHTING.

MASTER SHOT: see SHOT.

MATTE: A mask which obstructs some of the light passing through the camera lens. It can be of a specific shape (e.g. a keyhole) which is imposed on the film as a blank area while the photographic images are being exposed. In silent days it was often left blank. Nowadays mattes are more often produced with laboratory techniques than with camera-mounted masks. See TRAVELING MATTE.

MEDIUM SHOT: see SHOT.

MISE-EN-SCÈNE: A term generally used in reference to the staging of a play or a film production—in considering as a whole the settings, the arrangements of the actors in relation to the setting, lighting, etc. Some critics use the concept of mise-en-scène to describe what goes on *within the frame* in contrast with cutting, as the two key approaches to filmmakers' styles.

MONTAGE: In Russia, montage meant DYNAMIC CUTTING; in Europe, the term is equivalent to editing; in Hollywood, it is used more specifically to describe a sequence using rapid SUPERIMPOSITIONS, JUMP-CUTS, and DISSOLVES in order to create a kind of kaleidoscopic effect.

MOVING SHOT: see SHOT.

OPTICALS: SPECIAL EFFECTS usually created in the laboratory with an optical printer, but most of them can also be created in the camera. These include most TRANSITIONS (dissolve, fade, iris, wipe). See, for example, MATTE, SUPERIMPOSITION, and TRAVELING MATTE.

PAN SHOT: see SHOT.

PARALLEL ACTION: An effect created by CROSS-CUTTING, which enables the viewer to be two or more places concurrently. Using parallel action, a filmmaker can extend or condense REAL TIME and create a SCREEN TIME with a logic of its own. For instance, if the filmmaker wants to lengthen the suspense while the heroine has one minute to answer a question on a TV quiz show, he can cut between the homes of anxious friends watching in four different cities.

REACTION SHOT: A CUTAWAY shot of a person reacting to the main action as listener or spectator. Some comedians have planned reaction shots to jokes in order to give the audience a chance to laugh without missing the next line.

REAL TIME: The actual time an action would need to occur; as opposed to SCREEN TIME, a principal aesthetic effect created by filmmakers in transforming reality into art. Real time is preserved within the scenes of a play but (usually) only within the individual shots of a film.

REAR PROJECTION: A technique whereby the actors, sets, and props in front of the camera are combined with a background which consists of a translucent screen on which a picture (moving or still) is projected from behind. Almost always used when a scene takes place inside a moving vehicle. The actors sit still and the scenery they are supposedly passing by is projected behind them. Sometimes called "back projection" or "process shot."

REVERSE-ANGLE SHOT: see SHOT.

SCENE: see UNITS OF FILM LENGTH.

SCREEN DIRECTION: Whichever direction, left or right, the actor or object is looking at or moving toward, described from the *audience point of view*.

SCREEN TIME: Duration of an action as manipulated through editing, as opposed to REAL TIME. A principal aesthetic effect by which the filmmaker transforms reality into art. CUTAWAYS and INSERT SHOTS are two ways of stretching or condensing real time to give the film different time. If we cut between a race and the spectators' reactions, we often lengthen the actual time of the race. If we cut away for part of a movement, when we cut back we may have cut out a large chunk of the action. For other ways of manipulating time see: FAST and SLOW MOTION, CROSS-CUTTING, HIDDEN CUT, JUMP-CUTS, and PARALLEL ACTION.

SEPARATION: Shooting people in separate shots who are actually quite close together. A conversation may be filmed with one person looking right in MEDIUM SHOT and the other looking left in CLOSE-UP (probably after a TWO-SHOT establishing their nearness). A unique tool of cinema which can bring people in closer relation than if they were in the same shot.

SEQUENCE: see UNITS OF FILM LENGTH.

SHOT: A piece of film that has been exposed, without cuts or interruptions, in a single running of the camera. The shot is the elemental division of a film. Shots may be categorized: (1) according to the *distance* between the camera and its subject (e.g., a long shot)—these designations vary among directors and are relative to the size of the subject filmed and the way distances have been established in the film; (2) according to the *angle* of the camera in relation to the subject (e.g., a high-angle shot); (3) according to the *content,* nature or subject matter of what is being filmed (e.g., a reaction shot or a two-shot); or (4) according to the means by which the shot is accomplished physically (e.g., a tracking shot).

(1) LONG SHOT (LS): The camera seems to be at a distance from the subject being filmed.

MEDIUM SHOT (MS): A shot intermediate in distance between a long and a close shot.

CLOSE-UP (CU): The camera seems very close to the subject, so that when the image is projected most of the screen will be taken up with revealing a face and its expressions, or a plate of stew.

EXTREME CLOSE-UP (ECU): The camera seems very close to what would ordinarily be a mere detail in a close-up. For example, the whole screen is taken up with a shot of a tear welling up in an eye.

(2) HIGH-ANGLE SHOT: A shot which looks down on the subject from a height.

LOW-ANGLE SHOT: A shot which looks up at the subject.

EYE-LEVEL SHOT: Guess.

REVERSE-ANGLE SHOT: Shot taken by a camera positioned opposite (about 180°) from where the previous shot was taken. A reverse angle of a dog walking toward the camera would be a shot of it walking directly away from the camera. If a reverse-angle is made of two people in a TWO SHOT, the rules of CROSSING THE AXIS have to be observed by reversing their positions.

(3) ESTABLISHING SHOT: Often the opening shot of a sequence, showing the location of a scene or the arrangement of its characters. Usually a LONG SHOT. For example, if the story jumps from lover's lane, where an athelete is breaking training on the night before the big game, to his disastrous fumble at the championship, we will probably see the stadium and teams from a HIGH-ANGLE LONG SHOT before we close in on the hero's actions. Compare SLOW DISCLOSURE.

MASTER SHOT: Single shot of an entire piece of dramatic action. A standard Hollywood practice that facilitates the editing of a scene. For example, a conversation is likely to be photographed first as one lengthy TWO-SHOT; then it will be reshot in pieces at the different distances and angles needed to construct the scene.

TWO-SHOT. Close-up of two persons.

THREE-SHOT. Close-up of three persons.

(4) CIRCULAR CAMERA MOVEMENT: A camera movement that travels around its more or less stationary subject.

DOLLY or TRUCKING SHOT: One in which the camera *moves bodily* from one place to another. (Compare pan and tracking shots.)

MOVING SHOT: One taken from some normally moving object such as a plane or a car.

PAN SHOT: One during which the camera stays in one place but *rotates horizontally* on its axis.

SWISH PAN: A pan so rapid that the image appears blurred. It usually begins and ends at rest.

TILT SHOT: One in which the camera pivots along a *vertical* plane.

TRACKING SHOT: A dolly shot in which the camera moves *parallel* with its moving subject. If the camera moves in on a seated person, that is a dolly-in; if it travels alongside of a person walking down the block, that is a tracking shot.

ZOOM SHOT: A shot taken with a zoom lens (i.e., a lens which makes it possible to move visually toward or away from a subject without moving the camera). We can get closer to a subject with either a dolly or zoom shot. When we dolly into a subject, objects pass by the camera, giving a feeling of depth. When we zoom, the sensation is two-dimensional, much like coming close to a still photograph. Zooms are used a lot in covering football games.

SLOW DISCLOSURE: A shot starting in CLOSE-UP that does not reveal the location of the subject at first. It then moves back or cuts to a full revelation of the geography, which comes as a surprise. A shot typical of cartoons would show an animal sleeping comfortably and then zoom out to reveal that his enemy is lowering an axe over his head.

SLOW MOTION: Opposite of FAST MOTION. The action appears slower on the screen than it could in reality. Popular for dream and romantic effects, and to show the gracefulness of athletes.

SOFT FOCUS: see FOCUS.

SPECIAL EFFECTS: Visual special effects are OPTICALS.

STOCK FOOTAGE: Footage borrowed from previous films or a stock library. It is often newsreel footage of famous people and events or battle scenes and other hard to shoot footage.

STOP MOTION: The method by which trick photography is effected; the film is exposed one frame at a time, allowing time for rearrangement of models, etc., between shots and thus giving the illusion of motion by something normally inanimate. This is how *King Kong* was filmed and also how flowers can grow, bloom, and die within a few minutes. Stop motion applied to objects is *animation,* applied to people is *pixilation.*

SUBJECTIVE SHOT: Shot that seems to represent the point of view of a character in the story. It may be what he sees (e.g., a shot through the keyhole he is peeking through into the next room), or how he sees it (e.g., a blurred shot looking up at the surgeon from the operating table as the character awakes from anaesthesia). In *The Cabinet of Dr. Caligari,* we learn at the end of the film that the distorted, EXPRESSIONISTIC, MISE-EN-SCÈNE reflects the fact that the film's narrator is a mental patient.

SUPERIMPOSITION: An OPTICAL effect in which two or more images are on one piece of film, so that there appears to be a multiple exposure. Can be used when two characters played by the same actor have to meet; also for DISSOLVES, dream sequences, etc.

SWISH PAN: see SHOT.

SYNC or SYNCHRONISM: The relation between picture and sound. If they don't match, the film is said to be "out of sync." Easiest to spot by watching a person's lips as he speaks.

TAKE: see UNITS OF FILM LENGTH.

THREE-SHOT: see SHOT.

TILT SHOT: see SHOT.

TRACKING SHOT: see SHOT.

TRANSITIONS: Means of connecting two shots. The following transitions can be created either in the laboratory with an OPTICAL printer or in the camera.

DISSOLVE: The merging of the end of one shot with the beginning of the next; as the second shot becomes distinct, the first slowly fades away. Thus, for a while two images are SUPERIMPOSED. Also called "lap dissolves" and, in England, "mixes."

FADE: A fade-in shot begins in darkness and gradually assumes full brightness. A fade-out shot gradually gets darker.

IRIS: An iris-in shot opens from darkness into an expanding circle within which is the image. An iris-out is the opposite.

WIPE: A transition in which the second shot appears and "pushes" off the first one; usually they are separated by a visible vertical line, but the variations of wipes are many. Unlike an iris, there is a picture on both sides of the dividing line.

TRAVELING MATTE: A SPECIAL EFFECT used to blend actors in the studio with location or trick scenes. The actor is photographed against a dark background and this image can later be combined optically with the desired background. Thus actors can move among animated monsters, exploding shells, or cobras. The traveling matte is therefore unlike REAR PROJECTION.

TWO-SHOT: see SHOT.

UNITS OF FILM LENGTH:

FRAME: The individual picture on a strip of film. Sound films project 24 frames per second.

SHOT: A piece of film that has been exposed without cuts or interruptions. (Defined in detail under its own alphabetical listing.)

TAKE: Each performance of a piece of action in front of a camera (from "lights, camera, action!" to "cut!"). Each recording is numbered sequentially, until the director feels he has satisfactory results. From the takes he chooses one for each shot.

SCENE and SEQUENCE: Although the terms are used constantly, there is no agreement on what these units comprise. One definition is that a scene is determined by unity of time and place (like a dramatic scene) whereas a sequence is determined by unity of action (a more filmic unit).

WIPE: see TRANSITIONS.

ZOOM SHOT: see SHOT.

Index

CPSIA information can be obtained
at www.ICGtesting.com
Printed in the USA
BVHW040206061021
618252BV00017B/623

9 780231 054775